Grandparent Power!

Other books by Dr. Kornhaber

Grandparents-Grandchildren: The Vital Connection
(Coauthor, Kenneth L. Woodward)

Between Parents & Grandparents

Spirit

Grandparent —Power!—

*How to Strengthen the
Vital Connection Among Grandparents,
Parents, and Children*

Arthur Kornhaber, M.D.,
with Sondra Forsyth

Crown Publishers, Inc., New York

Published by Crown Publishers, Inc., 201 East 50th Street
New York, New York 10022. Member of the Crown
Publishing Group.

Random House, Inc. New York, Toronto, London, Sydney,
Auckland

CROWN is a trademark of Crown Publishers, Inc.

Manufactured in the United States

Design by Cynthia Dunne

Library of Congress Cataloging-in-Publication Data
Kornhaber, Arthur.
    Grandparent Power!:how to strengthen the vital
  connection among grandparents, parents, and children/
  Arthur Kornhaber, with Sondra Forsyth.—1st ed.
      p.   cm.
    Includes bibliographical references and index.
    1. Grandparent and child.   2. Intergenerational
  relations.
    I. Forsyth, Sondra.   II. Title.
    HQ759.9.K66   1994
    306.874'5—dc20   94-8846
                                                   CIP

ISBN 0-517-59805-1

10   9   8   7   6   5   4   3   2   1

First Edition

With great respect, I dedicate this book to the emotionally and spiritually gifted grandparents who listened to their inner drive to keep families united, and thus pioneered the Grandparent Movement in America. It has been my privilege to know them and to learn from them over the years. With courage, dedication, and vitality, they paved the way so that future generations of grandparents could be empowered to improve the quality of life for their children and their children's children. God bless them all.

Contents

Grandparent Power!

Introduction

THE CHALLENGES OF GRANDPARENTING TODAY

The impetus for this book dates back to discoveries I began making in 1972. As a child psychiatrist in private practice, I had often found that treating an individual youngster really meant treating the whole family. Using a traditional psychiatric approach, I would frequently confer with the brothers, sisters, and parents of a troubled youth in order to piece together the child's world.

Yet in the course of lining up these family members, I began to have a nagging feeling that something—or someone—was being ignored in the traditional psychiatric family roll call. I turned to my young patients themselves to solve the mystery, and I quickly realized that there were indeed some vital people missing from the prescribed kinship assembly. I also learned, however, that these people were certainly not missing from the hearts and minds and souls of the youngsters in question. In fact, the children greatly loved and admired these people and sometimes they turned out to be the most important people in the children's lives. Who were these "mystery" people, adored by children but ignored by traditional psychiatry? The grandparents, of course.

Excited by my discovery, I began to talk with my patients' grandparents. Over and over, I heard people tell me they were "crazy" about their grandchildren. No matter how troubled the youngsters were, their grandparents were hard put to stop waxing eloquent about them. All of the wonderful things these people were saying made me think back to my own childhood, when my grandparents and I had reveled in each other's company. We, too, had been "crazy" about one another. I began to wonder why the grandparent/grandchild bond was overlooked by the mental health profession. Why was family therapy so frequently a two-generational process?

Intrigued by this question, I decided to take a systematic, scientific approach to learn more about what I have come to call the "vital connection" between grandparents and grandchildren. I started the Grandparent Study, a longitudinal research project. During the course of my work, I came across many grandparents who were enjoying their grandchildren to the fullest and who were happy with the balance they had achieved in their lives between family and work. However, I also met many more grandparents who loved their grandchildren deeply, but who felt frustrated in trying to find that balance, largely because the unprecedented health and fitness of today's new breed of grandparents often translates into an active lifestyle which is not at all what most people had anticipated at this stage in their lives. The elders of the 1990s are in effect emotional pioneers as they wrestle with the conflicts between their personal needs and those of their grandchildren. As one woman said, "I'm a fifty-five-year-old single grandmother with a very demanding career as an advertising executive. I started working when my own kids were preschoolers, right after my divorce, but at least I saw them mornings, evenings, and weekends. As a working grandmother, though, I feel as if I'm not involved with my two-year-old grandson at all. I certainly don't have the time to baby-sit very often. On the other hand, when I do baby-sit, I put on my sneakers and keep up with him just fine. In a funny way, I feel younger now than I have in years. I work out at the gym, I eat right, and menopause has been no big deal. I thought I'd be a little old lady knitting booties in a rocking chair at this point, and now it looks as though I won't even approach that image until I'm a great-grandmother—if ever! Anyway, I find this very confusing. I don't have any model as to how to be a good grandmother and still be *me*."

This woman is far from alone in her concerns. However, for some grandparents, an even more central issue is coping with the unexpected vagaries of today's complex and pressured society. One grandfather summed up the problem when he pleaded, "Tell me how to be a good grandparent today. I haven't got a clue. I mean, I always thought I'd be the wise elder, but things are changing so fast that I feel like my experience counts for nothing. I'm not *that* old—sixty-two next month—but just in my lifetime, all the rules have changed. We've got working mothers, day care, divorces right and left, legal abortions, kids doing drugs, violence in the streets. And the economy is a mess. My daughter and her husband just moved halfway across the country so he could take a better-paying job. My wife and I are heartbroken because now we'll hardly ever see the grandchildren. This isn't the way I thought things would be at all. I guess Grandma and Grandpa are pretty much out of the picture these days. Am I right?"

Sadly, the answer in many cases is yes. Even our legal system fails to recognize grandparents as "real family." In fact, the whole nonparental cast of family characters has been reduced to bit players, when they really should be given major roles. One example of this is the fact that unless a specific family has made other arrangements, children who are orphaned will automatically become wards of the state, and then grandparents will have to apply formally through social service agencies in order to become foster parents to their own flesh and blood. For that matter, grandparents are not even allowed to take an ill or injured grandchild to a hospital emergency room without a signed release from the parents.

Laws, of course, can't regulate feelings. A recent survey of about 45,000 first- through sixth-graders by *Weekly*

Reader revealed that if children were in charge of planning family vacations, their first choice would be to go to Grandma and Grandpa's house. My research corroborates this finding. As far as youngsters are concerned, Grandma and Grandpa are definitely not "out of the picture." In fact, my study showed that the grandparent/grandchild bond is second only in emotional importance to the parent/child bond. I published my findings in *Grandparents-Grandchildren: The Vital Connection,* which I wrote with my good friend Kenneth Woodward of *Newsweek* magazine, and I published further findings in a second book, *Between Parents & Grandparents.* These books opened a Pandora's box of issues for many people. I was flooded with questions from all parts of the country. Every published review of my books resulted in fifty letters to me. Every interview produced a hundred more. Parents and grandparents alike called at all hours of the day and night with a surprising variety of questions, concerns, and problems. Obviously, many grandparents and grandchildren were not getting enough of one another's love. Over and over, I heard people puzzling about how they could be closer to their grandchildren. All of these people were struggling with one basic issue—how to maintain the "vital connection" in today's times.

I was taken aback at the enormity of the response. My books had clearly hit a nerve. Scores of people were coming to me with questions that were apparently not being answered anywhere else. "At last, someone to talk to" were the first words uttered by a grandmother from Mississippi when I answered her phone call. After that, a look at the child-care section of a major bookstore further convinced me that I had more work to do. There were books on every conceivable aspect of child rearing and family life, from general ones like Dr. Spock's classic to very specific subjects such as breast-feeding, adoption, cesarean sections, and stepfamilies. But there was not one how-to manual for grandparents. Had the "extended family" slipped so far from our collective consciousness that we were leaving each new generation of nuclear families all alone to reinvent the nurturing of our children? I found this astonishing in light of the fact that throughout history, grandparents have been the key to family harmony and continuity. They have always served as long-term repositories of information—how to outlast a dry season, what herbs to use for medicinal purposes, methods of child rearing. Their wisdom and experience contributed in very real terms to the basic physical survival of primitive cultures. As teachers, supporters of parents, historians, nurturers, consultants, and even entertainers, their psychological, social, and spiritual functions were of paramount importance. I wondered how our society had possibly come to dismiss this powerful, multifaceted grandparent role.

In the meantime, letters kept pouring in, begging for affirmation, information, and guidance about grandparenting in these turbulent times. I began seriously to consider writing a third grandparenting book. But first, I felt the need to focus on the work of the Foundation for Grandparenting, which I established with my wife Carol in 1980. The stated mission of the Foundation is to "raise people's awareness about the importance of grandparenting for all three generations." In addition to the many programs we have started and the grandparent/grandchild summer camp we run, we also publish a newsletter, *Vital Connections,* which serves as the voice of our grandparent network. The addresses for these organizations and publications—along with many more which also serve the needs of grandparents—are listed in the appendix of this book.

In the course of my work, as I continued to explore the depth of love and joy that grandparents and grandchildren have for one another, I made another discovery. I slowly began to realize that this bond is much deeper and more potent than even I had anticipated. I know now that it reaches beyond the biological, psychological, and social boundaries that modern science uses to explain such things. This attachment contains what I believe is the most basic, purest form of human love, an unconditional love that is rooted deeply in the human spirit. As one grandmother said, "It's made in heaven." I began to realize that the grandparent/grandchild connection, for both elders and children, creates a happiness which contributes significantly to the health and well-being of both generations. Beyond that, I saw that the love between a grandparent and grandchild has the capacity to illuminate and transform people and literally to give meaning to life. The recognition of this spiritual dimension of the relationship explained to me why people experience such deep joy when this "vital connection" is fulfilled, and such profound pain when it is severed.

As I traveled all over the country doing research, speaking to audiences, and being involved in the national campaign to gain visitation rights for disenfranchised grandparents, I found that my belief in the importance of grandparenting was confirmed. I witnessed how strongly grandparenting issues are a part of everyday life, and how they are very much in the minds and hearts of all people. I saw many grandparents loving their families, enjoying the good times, and helping in times of stress. I became more and more aware of the power that grandparents possess to make their families happy and to bring order and meaning to the family structure. Everywhere I went, I met people who had these vital connections, people for whom grandparenting was an almost inexpressibly joyful and meaningful role. For many of these fulfilled grandparents, their grandparenthood is, as one grandmother said, "what my life is all about." For these people, the good they confer as grandparents is reflected not only in their grandchildren but in their own children too.

At the same time I was also encountering another scenario: children, parents, and grandparents fervently wanting to be closer. One especially moving experience was to change the course of my work for the next several years. I was addressing a gathering of more than four hundred parents at a luncheon in a large Western city. The audience was composed mostly of transplanted Easterners. I was talking about the "unconditional love" factor in the grandparent/grandchild relationship, and suddenly one young woman in the audience popped out of her chair and, with tears running down her cheeks, said: "I understand what you're saying. I agree with you completely. But what can I do? My husband was transferred out here and my parents and his parents are still back in Boston. My kids are missing out on so much. This is just killing me!"

A great affirmative murmur rose in the audience. "Yes, yes," I heard from the group. I told the young woman that if she waited until after my speech, I would be happy to talk with her. Well, she did wait—along with more than two hundred others! This get-together was one of the most moving encounters I have ever had. There wasn't a dry eye in the place. The experience showed me that not only were grandchildren and grandparents suffering as a result of grandparent deprivation, but that the middle generation was suffering too.

At that moment, I knew without question that I had to write another book. While *Grandparents-Grandchildren: The Vital Connection* and *Between Parents & Grandparents* had been important as theoretical, analytical descriptions of grandparenting, a different kind of book was needed—one that would continue to raise people's grandparenting "consciousness" but which would offer some practical, hands-on, nuts-and-bolts information about how to grandparent. There was a need for a concrete guidebook to help people understand the importance of grandparenting not only for the sake of their families and society as a whole, but also as a heretofore underestimated step in human development. To be the best grandparent possible, people do need to know how to navigate uncharted waters. But today's grandparents must also come to appreciate the full extent of their potential to grow as human beings. Only then can they truly influence their families for the better, and inspire and educate the younger generations so that they will have the strength to conquer society's current ills and move toward a better tomorrow—one in which they will have a template for how to make their own grandparenthood the vital life stage it is meant to be.

This book is my answer to that need—a need which is heightened by the sheer number of grandparents in this country today. There are more than 60 million at this writing. And as the members of the huge postwar baby-boom generation move past midlife, the ranks of grandparents will swell so that by the time the '90s draw to a close, ushering in the twenty-first century, the number of grandparents in America will have grown to more than 90 million.

If you are—or will be—one of them, then you surely have questions and concerns which no other generation before you has had to grapple with. That's why this book was written. I have set out to help and encourage you as you change the very definitions of the roles of matriarch and patriarch, and to cheer you on as you relish the age-old pleasures of grandparenting and simultaneously face the unprecedented challenges of being the elder population in our ever-changing society. In the pages that follow, I will address your various dilemmas. I will help you to get in touch with the strength of your growing wisdom and experience, help you to understand how the grandparent/grandchild connection nourishes your body and soul, and help you to begin to savor the importance of your special kind of love in the lives of your grandchildren. Perhaps most exciting of all, I will help you understand how important the force of grandparenting can be in your own life. Far from a period of stagnation and eventual decline, your grandparent years are destined to be a time of expansion, usefulness, and great joy.

This book is a celebration of that joy—but most of all of the *power* of being a grandparent today. Infused with all that you have become and are still becoming, your grandchildren will have a good chance to grow up to be all they can be. Surely that is the most enduring legacy you can leave to these precious youngsters who stand to inherit the world in the millennium to come.

Arthur Kornhaber, M.D.
December 1993

PART ONE

What's So Grand About Grandparenting?

1

The Birth of a Grandparent

There is a famous Norman Rockwell painting, circa 1940, depicting Thanksgiving dinner: a plump, apple-cheeked, gray-haired Grandma and a balding, bespectacled Grandpa are presiding over the family feast, with children and grandchildren gathered together to savor not just the turkey and the pumpkin pie but the feeling of continuity and safety and belonging. The message is clear and comforting: *This is our family. These are our elders. This is how we do things. This is where we matter very much, and where we get the strength and self-esteem and pride we need to carry on.*

It's certainly no secret that this reassuring scene is not all that common these days. With the divorce rate at 55 percent and climbing, and with the middle generation moving in search of education and employment while the elder generation continues working or retires to the Sunbelt in unprecedented numbers, the likelihood of gathering an intact three- or four-generation family around a holiday table is fairly slim. And getting that multigenerational family to interact easily and lovingly on a regular basis takes a lot of doing. Ironically, however, that kind of interaction is precisely what people desperately need in these chaotic and stressful times. Nuclear families—the truncated Mom/Dad/kids version of kinship which has become the accepted model in this country—are hard-pressed to cope alone. Several factors have contributed to this modern notion of what constitutes a family, and to the resulting problems. For one thing, there has been a trend in psychological circles to blame parents, particularly mothers, for people's problems, thus encouraging young adults to embrace the idea of getting away from the family of origin in order to achieve independence, a goal which oftens turns out to be a Pyrrhic victory—that is, one beset by staggering losses. There has also been a glamorization of the nuclear family and a simultaneous ridiculing of in-laws by Hollywood and other media. But perhaps most significant was the invention of the suburbs and single-family homes after World War II. As James Kunstler, author of *The Geography of Nowhere,* points out, the "so-called American dream of a split-level on a half an acre" has become a nightmare. He writes that "the living arrangements Americans think of as normal come loaded with hidden costs—fiscal, social and spiritual."

Exacerbating the problem, of course, is the fact that in most cases today, both parents work in the outside world and quality child care is difficult to come by. More and more young parents are struggling to perform the difficult juggling act of keeping their marriages healthy, holding on to their jobs, and rearing their children—all at the same time. Meanwhile the older generation, whether by choice or by chance, is increasingly isolated from the lives of children and grandchildren.

Yet if that's the bad news, the good news is this: While we can't turn back the clock to that idyllic Norman Rockwell Thanksgiving, we *can* begin to work right now to overcome current social obstacles, reconnect our families in innovative ways, and look to a bright future. What's so exciting is that the power to do all that lies as surely with grandparents today as it has since the dawn of humankind. Yes, there have been myriad changes in our society even within recent memory, but these changes are merely cultural. They have nothing to do with the deep and abiding instincts people have always had to be joyful as a family, to protect their own, and to ensure the survival of the next generation.

I know, however, that you may not feel ready to meet the challenges of becoming an in-law, and then a grandparent, particularly if there has been only a brief time since your youngest child left home, or if there are children still living with you. Research shows there is an optimum time to "notch up" to this next stage of life, ideally after an "empty nest" break of about five years. This allows for a respite from raising your own children and lets you fulfill whatever personal needs and dreams you've had to put on hold while bringing up your family. After this period of rest and renewal, you'll have the emotional strength to handle the demands and savor the pleasures of grandparenting.

Of course, you can't dictate what your children do, and especially if a child gets pregnant as a teenager and decides to have the baby, you'll be caught unaware before your grandparenting instincts are in gear. In such a situation, you will simply have to muster your resources to cope with the responsibilities at hand. Still, the idea is to encourage your children to grow up a little before they marry and have children. The whole family will benefit. The Grandparent Project has shown how well families function when both parents and grandparents have matured so that the child has grown out of the hostile-dependent phase of her relationship with parents and has achieved psychological adulthood, and at the same time the elders have recouped their inner energies and are ready to focus on family concerns again.

Of course, not only does the grandparent role bring new responsibilities, but it is also a breathtaking reminder that you are growing old, no matter how active you are or how young you feel. Rest assured that you are not alone if you are having trouble accepting the advent of this new phase of your life. I can also guarantee, though, that once the baby is born, your misgivings will yield to an unparalleled joy that will literally transform you. The proof of this is easy to come by. All we have to do is listen to the voices of grandparents as they speak about what they felt at the very moment the first grandchild was born. Here are two of them:

> Marlene, a top-flight magazine editor, was in a meeting when the phone call came. Trim and attractive at fifty-five, she had been intent on going

over sales figures and advertising revenue with the publisher. "I had closed my office door and instructed Linda, my secretary, not to let anyone interrupt us except in an emergency," she told me. "That's why I was startled when Linda buzzed me. What could possibly be so important?"

The answer, as it turned out, was that Marlene's only child, Jennifer, had given birth to her first child prematurely. "My son-in-law was on the line, so excited he could barely talk straight," Marlene remembers. "He and Jennifer had gone away for a long weekend, sort of a last vacation before becoming parents, and Jennifer had gone into labor unexpectedly. The whole thing had happened really fast, so Ron hadn't even gotten a chance to call me until it was all over. He was saying, 'It's a boy! Five pounds, two ounces and perfect! Jennifer's fine! We're all fine!'

"Tears just started streaming down my face. I had a grandchild! For some reason, I got this mental image of a horizon, like life stretching out farther than I could ever see. Then everything about the miracle of Jennifer's birth came back to me with the most amazing clarity, and immediately I had a jumble of memories from her baby years on. I could actually smell that special scent of a baby. It isn't powder or lotion. It absolutely comes with the baby. And there's the way babies curl their little fists around your finger and grip so hard you can't believe it . . . and the way they crow . . . and when they smile at you, it is the most insanely flattering thing in the whole world.

And I remember thinking, My little Jennifer is a mother, and I'm a grandmother! I had been sure I was ready for the big event, but the truth is that nothing could have prepared me for the rush of emotions I felt at the moment when I first knew I was really a grandmother. For one thing, I had a visceral need to hold that baby, to connect with him, to let him know that he's a part of me and I'm a part of him, and that I'll always love him and be there for him. But the craziest thing was that I wanted to live forever, so I could see him grow up—and *help* him grow up! There was so much I wanted to tell him. And then I remembered a quote I had read from child advocate Neil Postman: 'Children are living messages we send to a time we will never see.' For the first time in my life I really knew the meaning of the word 'spiritual.' That night, I walked outside and looked at the heavens and I felt as though I was seeing the stars for the first time."

Ruth, age sixty, has always been a full-time homemaker. She's been married to Sam for thirty years, and they've reared four children in the small Missouri town where he works for the post office. "Our second son, Jimmy, was the first to get married," Ruth said. "He had gone to the University of Michigan and he started living with a girl during his junior year. We never met her or her parents. They're divorced and the father lives in Hawaii and the mother lives in Seattle. They've apparently never been very involved with the girl since she went away to school. Jimmy and the girl—her name is Mary Ann—went to a justice of the peace after graduation. They both got scholarships to graduate school.

"Well, anyway, they called that summer to say that Mary Ann was pregnant, and they said they wanted me to start saving so I could fly to Ann Arbor when the baby was due and take the childbirth classes and be one of Mary Ann's 'labor coaches.' I thought they were nuts! I had been knocked out every time I gave birth, and I just couldn't picture being in the delivery room with this daughter-in-law I didn't even know. But I'll make a long story short. Sam and I both decided to go. I got there about three weeks before Mary Ann was due, and Sam took two weeks plus his unused sick days and arrived about a week before she was due. We were all living in their little campus apartment and we sure got to know each other. Seriously, we were a little standoffish at first, but then it was great. Jimmy insisted that I had to show Mary Ann my fried chicken method, and she loved hearing me tell her about when Jimmy and the other kids were little.

"But the best thing we did was talk about grandparents. We talked about Mary Ann's grandparents and my own grandparents, and Sam's, too. We talked about what kind of grandparents Mary Ann and Jimmy wanted their child to have. Sam and I told them what kind of grandparents we would like to be. I was surprised at Sam. He usually isn't all that talkative, but he sure went on about being a grandfather! I started to see him as a different man. And I started looking forward to knowing him as a grandfather. Because he sure never treated his kids the way he talked about treating his grandchildren.

"So then, three days after her due date, she went into labor, and she was really good with the breathing they had taught her. I was very impressed. The labor moved along pretty quickly for a first baby, and after we got to the hospital, the baby started crowning before we knew it. Jimmy and Sam and I were hugging each other and laughing and crying at the same time, and Mary Ann was pushing and then just like that, it happened. The baby slipped out right into Jimmy's arms, and she let out a wail like you wouldn't believe. I swear, I felt like I saw a glow around her—a light that had come into the world. And she looked exactly like my babies had looked, except she had a whole bunch of dark hair, just like her mother. This little baby—she came from all of us! And in just an instant, everything was changed. Jimmy was a daddy, and Sam and I were still his parents, but not the same. I can't quite explain it. I've never been that good with words. But do you get what I mean? It's like we moved up. We became the grandparents. And I was squeezing Sam's arm so hard, and he whispered, 'I love you, Grandma.' And then the doctor was finished with the baby and he handed her to Mary Ann. Mary Ann said, 'Her name is Hope,' and Hope started nursing and I just thought, Oh, please God, let the world be a good place for my granddaughter to grow up in."

Obviously, Marlene and Ruth lead quite different lives, and so do their children. Yet their reactions to the miracle of the birth of a grandchild are strikingly similar. As Marlene said, "You must really think I'm a sentimental old fool. But David is five now, and his younger brother, Bobby, is three. They have changed my life. Oh, I haven't retired yet, and I still work impossibly hard, but grandchildren have given me a new focus. They are a new generation, and that means terrific stuff like wonder and curiosity and discovery. And joy. Don't forget that. That's a rare commodity these days. And I get only the good parts. I mean, Jennifer and Ron are in charge of the toilet training and tantrums, and I'm in charge of the treats and tall tales. Now *that's* a good deal!"

Marlene, of course, is not a "sentimental old fool." Sentiment is nothing to be embarrassed about, and if it is more the province of grandparents than of anyone else, that should make us feel proud and privileged, not foolish. Marlene needs to relinquish the negative stereotypes of older people being maudlin and let herself experience fully the powerful instincts that have linked generations since the beginning of the human race. When she goes on and on about her grandchildren, she is simply singing what some cultures call the Grandmother's Song. Each grandmother's variation is unique, imbued with the magic of her own joys and sorrows, and yet the theme is common to all: "I am your heritage and you are my legacy. We are part of a chain. Come to me for the wisdom of my experience and for my love that knows no bounds. Let me come to you for the newness of your experience and for your love that knows no bounds."

Yet while the essence of grandparenthood—for both

grandmothers and grandfathers—remains a constant across time and place, the day-to-day reality of the role varies widely. As I have said, this is nowhere truer than in contemporary America, where the social fabric is being woven and unraveled and rewoven with unforeseen speed. Marlene, for example, in spite of the fact that she's an instinctively wonderful grandmother—what I call a "natural"—is not at all like the grandma in the Rockwell painting. For one thing, Marlene has been divorced since her daughter was twelve. For another, she has always worked outside the home. And she certainly doesn't look like a Rockwell grandma. Thanks to a prudent diet, a regular exercise routine, and a good hair colorist, Marlene is a stunning woman who wears tailored suits to work, and jeans and T-shirts on weekends. She has her own apartment and a busy social life that includes women friends, couples, and—as of about three months ago—a new man in her life.

But, yes, Marlene "does Thanksgiving," as she puts it—except only every third year. "Ron's parent's, who are in fact a very 'traditional' set of grandparents, had all of us over last year," she explained to me. "The year before that, Jennifer and Ron and the kids went to my ex-husband's house. He's remarried and they have his wife's two kids and two of their own. So now this year, it's my turn to have the family over. This setup is not at all what I had pictured years ago on my wedding day. But the grandchildren seem fine with it. Look, it's all they've ever known, so they think this is normal, I guess."

Marlene is probably right, particularly since she and the other adults in her splintered and restructured family are to be commended for making a concerted effort to normalize the situation as much as possible and to make the children a priority. Marlene and her family are certainly far from alone as they struggle to respond to the biological urge to maintain the vital grandparent/grandchild connection while social forces conspire to make that age-old human need difficult to fulfill. As Marlene confessed to me, "We sure could use some help."

I'll wager that you feel the same way. I say this because during more than twenty years of researching the special nature of the grandparent/grandchild connection, I've talked with scores of people from coast to coast and read countless heartfelt letters. What I've learned is that while the grandparenting instinct is as strong as ever, people of all generations are conflicted and worried and stymied as they try to let that basic drive go to work for them. That's because during our lifetime grandparenting has become increasingly complicated. In the past, grandparents were more or less the same from generation to generation and society had a place for them. Their roles in the family and their "jobs" in society were necessary and never questioned. There was little confusion about the privileges and responsibilities that went along with those roles. Grandparents were certain where they belonged in the family and in the world, and everyone else was comfortable with grandparents doing what they do. For the most part, people were as certain about the meaning of grandparenthood as they were about things like their marriages, their jobs, their government's policies, and their religious beliefs. But there are few such certainties in life right now. Because of the wild fluctuations that define our contemporary society, you have it much tougher than your forebears did. Even so, my long experience has taught me that you—as part of today's brave new breed of grandparents—are more than up to the challenge.

The Urge to Grandparent

For one thing, if you listen to your heart, you'll find that you know more than you think you do. The organically based urge to grandparent has strong biological, psychological, and emotional roots. It's part of the way you're made. You are linked genetically to your grandchildren just as surely as you are linked to your own children. The powerful urges to bond with a grandchild are part of a complex natural formula. True, there are factors which can affect your grandparenting urge—age, health, readiness, even personality and temperament. Nevertheless, your drive is there. Nature charges parents and grandparents with the responsibility for the survival of children. Besides love, a parent or grandparent feels the need to assure the survival of a child in part because the child carries the genetic legacy of the parent or grandparent. In effect, by assuring the survival of a child, a parent or grandparent ensures his or her own biological, genetic immortality.

What's Special About the Grandparent/Grandchild Connection

This basic biological urge to assure the survival of the child is something that grandparents and parents have in common. From there on, however, parents and grandparents have a very different experience with children, and frankly, grandparents get the best of it.

As you well know, most of the day-to-day responsibility for the survival of your children fell on your shoulders as a parent. On the other hand, as a grandparent you are exempt not only from the primary responsibility of raising your grandchildren, but also from much of the emotional fluctuation that is part of the package—for the simple reason that you are most likely not with your grandchildren twenty-four hours a day. As one grandmother said to me, "Timmy and Karen look forward to seeing me just as much as I look forward to seeing them. The car pulls up in front of my house and they practically tumble out and race up the walk and just about knock me over hugging me. What a feeling! The last time they came, they stayed the whole weekend and we baked cookies and planted bulbs and my husband told them ghost stories until all hours. Then, on Sunday, I dressed the kids up and took them to church and they were as good as gold. Their mother says they're never that good for her! Well, I guess this partly has to do with the fact that we all know there's a time limit. I can wink at having flour all over the kitchen for one weekend and they can sit still in church for one Sunday because it's not run-of-the-mill. I was much shorter with my own children. I know I was. And with your own kids, you're always worrying about their schooling and whether they get along with their friends and whether you can afford to give them every advantage. It's not that I don't have concerns about my grandchildren. I'd do anything for them. But I don't have to! That's the point. Their parents are the ones who are in charge. I'm off-duty on that score. So when I'm with the kids, it's practically a holiday."

What this woman is talking about is what we formally call "unconditional love"—or as near to it as human beings can get. This love lights the life of your grandchild, and your child too. The unique character of unconditional love was aptly described by Jean-Paul Sartre when he wrote, "I could make my grandmother go into raptures of joy just by being hungry." It is this pure kind of love which gives the grandparent/grandchild connection so much power.

It is pure because however it appears and evolves between two people, the emotional experience of love is quickly encumbered by their nature, their circumstances, and the world they inhabit. Love is always transfigured, for better or worse. The grandchild comes into the world with little such baggage, and the grandparents have hopefully lightened up their own. For them, a grandchild no longer represents their hopes and dreams as their own child did. For them the grandchild represents joy, renewal, and happiness. This is a secret they see in one another's eyes. While parents must temper their affection with lessons and discipline, either granting or withholding their love depending on the behavior of their children, grandparents can most often offer love with no strings attached.

Not only that, but children don't feel the psychological need to be different from their grandparents in the same way that they do from their parents. This means that there is much less potential for conflict between grandparents and grandchildren, even during the turbulent teenage years. Psychologically, children need to separate from their parents in order to become individuals in their own right. In a way, when this happens, the children relinquish part of their relationship with the parents—the part that involves the dependence of the children and the absolute authority of the parents. Yet because children don't feel the same urge to separate themselves from their grandparents, you will find that few of the emotional storms and power struggles that pepper the parent/child relationship happen between grandparents and grandchildren. This doesn't mean that you won't have problems or get caught in the crossfire occasionally, but the grandparent/grandchild relationship is largely free of the tensions that can characterize a parent/child relationship. In fact, you may well find that you remain something of an emotional sanctuary for your grandchildren, particularly during their adolescent stage. You may also be called upon to act as a referee between parents and children.

One grandfather told me about the time his sixteen-year-old grandson got arrested for shoplifting. "Scott's a good boy. He did it on a dare, and he knew it was stupid. He had never done anything like that before. He slipped some tapes of the Grateful Dead in his pocket and the security guard saw him do it and collared him. The other boys ran away and left him there. He was scared to death. The guard said he could call his parents, but he called me. He said, 'Grandpa, I'm in big trouble. You've got to help me. Mom and Dad will kill me!' Well, I heard him out, and I told him to put the guard on the phone, and I said I'd be right over. When I got there, Scott was trying not to cry. The guard was saying stuff about big fines and going to jail. I settled everything. I said it was a first offense and I would call my attorney if I had to, but I'd prefer to have the guard trust me. I said I could handle the boy, and make sure this never happened again. So the guy dropped the charges. Scott and I went back to my house, and then he did cry. And we never, ever told a soul. I didn't think we needed to. He learned his lesson and he knows he can count on me."

Yes, Scott can indeed count on his grandfather. That's what the special grandparent/grandchild connection is all about: unconditional love and support that are not forthcoming in quite the same way anywhere else. But just because that love is natural doesn't mean it will flower fully without some help. After all, the vital connection does not exist in a vacuum. In order to establish it and nurture it, you must also deal with the middle generation, and with extended family members such as the other grandparents and perhaps aunts, uncles, cousins, and stepparents. Given all of that, you are wise to lay the groundwork for good grandparenting as early as possible. In fact, the ideal time is long before the birth of your first grandchild. This involves being a positive influence in the lives of the parents-to-be. Remember that your child's marriage is the emotional soil in which your grandchildren grow and that if you delicately and respectfully garden that soil, with love and attention, you will help create the best conditions for a good crop of grandchildren—and a good relationship between yourself and the younger generations.

When Your Child Gets Engaged

Good grandparenting begins early, long before the birth of a grandchild. This is why you should make an effort to garden your child's relationship with the person he or she has chosen to marry during the courtship and engagement period. Obviously, your future son- or daughter-in-law will be the parent of your grandchildren-to-be. That means that the fate of your grandparenthood lies at least partly in that person's hands. Your children and children-in-law are the linchpins of the relationship between yourself and your grandchild, and they play a critical role in fostering—or hindering—that relationship.

Beyond that, legally, the parents of your grandchildren have all the rights and you have none. Your grandchildren are solely, in a sense, the property of their parents. In the best of all possible worlds, this unfortunate technicality would never come into play, but realistically, given the current divorce and remarriage rates, as unthinkable as it seems, you could find yourself at some time in the future battling with your grandchildren's parents for the right to stay a part of your grandchildren's lives. The surest way to avert such a tragedy is to establish a genuinely loving and respectful relationship with your children-in-law right from the beginning. And even if the worst-case scenario never happens and your extended family remains fairly blissfully intact, you're simply better off if you have a solid relationship with the whole cast of characters.

As with most things in life, that's easier said than done. Of course, if you actually like the prospective spouse and approve of the match, you're off to a wonderful start. But if you have misgivings about the impending marriage, you're going to have to call on all of your maturity, wisdom, and experience to handle the situation and come off as supportive and understanding. But it's well worth the effort, because what you do now sets the tone for the entire unfolding of the next chapter of your life. One grandfather who coped with such a situation is John, now fifty-five. Six years ago, his daughter got engaged to a man John didn't like at all.

"From the day the kids announced the engagement, John started worrying about how he could ever be a good grandfather because he couldn't stand Lou," John's wife, Linda, said. "But, being as smart and patient as he is, he worked it out."

John agreed. "It wasn't easy, but I had had a wonderful grandfather myself and I couldn't wait until I had grandchildren of my own. I didn't want anything to interfere with my chance to have a good relationship with them. I looked at the situation as a challenge. But I hated Lou's outlook, his friends, and his attitudes. In my eyes he had no saving graces. I just couldn't understand what my daughter saw in him. He didn't even have a job. I thought he was shiftless and lazy," John said.

"It took me five years, and a lot of fishing trips together, and a lot of biting my tongue, and praying. By the time the grandchildren were coming along, Lou and I were good friends, and wouldn't you know, he was working for me in my contracting business. Turns out he's a fine person and a hard worker. He just never had any guidance, it seems. Anyway, it was the fishing trips that got us so we could talk. I was looking for something that we had in common . . . a way to bridge the gap. The fish did it. And now we take the little ones fishing with us."

With his problem-solving attitude, John found a way to become a powerful grandparent. You can do that, too. Remember, the better you get along with your children and their spouses, the more you'll have the opportunity to love and cherish your grandchildren. So if a child-in-law makes a mistake or does something you don't like, don't hold grudges. We all makes mistakes, but that doesn't mean that we will keep repeating the same mistake over and over again. We can all learn and we can all change bad habits. Here are some concrete suggestions for establishing a sense of love and trust between you and your future child-in-law, and ensuring a chance to be a good grandparent.

Choose Your Battles

Obviously, the practice of arranging marriages has virtually disappeared from our culture, and with it any vestige of parental control over whom a child decides to wed. Add to that the fact that American youngsters are notoriously headstrong as adolescents, and that the majority live away from home during the college years, and you have a situation which may well mean that you won't even meet your future child-in-law until after the forthcoming nuptials are a fait accompli. Yet while this may not be the scenario you had once envisioned, you *can* learn to love and accept the person if you make an effort and refrain from hasty judgments. Keep in mind that you brought up your child, imparting values along the way, and now is the time to trust that you have done such a good job that he or she will make a wise choice.

As one mother said, "When my children were little, I somehow pictured them marrying people I knew, people from our community, the children of my close friends. I remember my next-door neighbor and I watching our kids play in the backyard wading pool one summer when they were all still preschoolers, and we were kind of joking about how her four-year-old son, Matthew, would be the perfect match for my three-year-old daughter, Jennifer. And then, right on cue, Matt and Jenny started fighting over a toy boat, and my neighbor and I were laughing and saying, yep, the perfect married couple. But I think underneath we did feel that our kids would pick people we were familiar with. Now this was in the early '70s, when everything was just starting to change, and over the years I went back to work, my neighbor got divorced and moved away, and our whole community was different, with latchkey kids and remarriages, and people getting transferred in and out so fast you hardly got to know them. By the time my kids were in high school, I barely knew any of the other families. So Jennifer brought home her first real date, for the homecoming dance the fall of her sophomore year, and he was a Japanese boy. Don't get me wrong. I'm not a bigot, but it was just a little bit of a shock. Of course, my husband and I—and *Sesame Street* and *Mr. Rogers*—are the ones who taught Jennifer to be tolerant. Anyway, it turned out that both of this boy's parents were physicians, a lovely family. And they were just as concerned as we were about the reality of the situation—you know, the challenges of an interracial relationship. But none of us got carried away. I mean, the kids were only fifteen. If they had been older and more serious, I think we would have talked to them about the future, about how this is not yet a perfect world when it comes to tolerance, and about the prejudice their children might face. But as it was, we just left them alone."

Wisely, the woman and her husband welcomed their daughter's boyfriend into their home and hearts, and when young love had spent its course, Jennifer broke up with this boy and began dating other people. Her mother says the first relationship was a genuinely positive one, that the boy was a polite and attentive suitor who bolstered Jennifer's self-esteem and gave her insight into his parents' culture, and that most important, Jennifer felt confident that her parents would not gratuitously disapprove of her eventual choice of a mate. "I guess we showed her we trusted her judgment," says the woman. "She's away at college now, and she calls and talks forever, asking my advice about this and that. We're very close. She says she's in no rush to get engaged, mostly because she sees all the divorces in our generation and she wants to look before she leaps. That has to be a good thing. But I feel sure that when she gets really involved with someone, she'll talk to her father and me and not be afraid we'll shoot somebody down or alienate anyone."

This case is a perfect example of laying the groundwork for good in-law relationships very early, being sure to look at the big picture and not quibble over issues that aren't worthy of a fight. In other words, if you don't like your future son-in-law's taste in clothes, but he doesn't drink or do drugs, bite your tongue and count your blessings.

Have a Series of Family Meetings to Establish the Ways in Which You All Hope to Interact

On the other hand, you *are* older and wiser and there is absolutely no reason not to have some input into the young people's relationship. The trick is to do this without seeming to be meddling. "I always thought my mother-in-law was the nosiest, pickiest person in the world," laughs one woman whose son is engaged. "Now *I'm* about to become a mother-in-law, and I'm finding it hard to keep my nose out of the kids' business." Actually, she shouldn't necessarily keep her nose entirely out of the kids' business. They could surely benefit from her advice and experience, and that of her husband as well. But getting your points across without making the youngsters defensive is hard to do.

My suggestion—and this has worked in my personal life as well as for people I have counseled—is to schedule family meetings, which should have an actual agenda. You don't have to bang a gavel on the table, and you can certainly keep a sense of humor during the proceedings and create a festive atmosphere by serving snacks or coffee and dessert. Even so, you should really cover certain potentially troublesome topics such as how the young couple plans to finance further education, who does or doesn't have a job and a sense of direction, where they plan to live and whether or not this is realistic financially, how they are envisioning taking care of children when they decide to become parents, and most of all, how you can help.

Many families today, out of economic necessity, are forming three- and four-generation households, and you might want to consider this option. There has been a lot of negative press about so-called boomerang children who leave for college and then end up right back home, often with a spouse and children, either because of unemployment or because salaries in entry-level jobs are so low. I wonder, however, if this trend may not be a blessing in disguise. Extended families can be a boon, especially for the children, and people have a way of working out their differences if they know they have no other alternative.

In any case, while you can't solve all problems in the abstract, you can definitely get the potentially problematic issues on the table and talk about ways to deal with them. To get an idea of what you might like to discuss, have a look at the premarital counseling questionnaires now offered by many churches and synagogues. These are typically exhaustive lists of what people should know about one another and their true goals and dreams before making the commitment to marriage. One of the best is the "Prepare/Enrich Marriage Inventory," developed some ten years ago by David H. Olson, Ph.D., a professor of Family Social Service at the University of Minnesota. "Prepare/Enrich" is now used by more than two thousand counselors across the country, and can predict with 85 percent accuracy whether couples will stay married.

If the idea of getting involved in your children's relationships makes you uncomfortable, remember that even though your children have grown up, you can still carry considerable authority as a parent. Only within recent memory in the Western world have parents abdicated— or been forced out of—the role of wise and beloved elder. I firmly believe that it is both your right and your responsibility to reclaim that role. Your children may seem to be pushing you away, but never have they needed you more.

Also, while there may be intergenerational confrontations that belie this, keep in mind that in the deepest sense, your children will always love you and need you. And I don't have to tell you that every parent remains concerned about his or her child no matter how old the child is. You are a parent forever, even after you become a grandparent. This gives you the mandate to share the wisdom and experience that you have accumulated throughout life. So persevere. If you are not blatantly bossy and if you keep the lines of communication open and show that you're a good listener, and that you're not a preacher but a teacher, you will win the young people's trust and you'll all stand to benefit—including your grandchildren-to-be. I'm not saying that this will be easy, but I promise that you will grow through the process. Of course, it does sometimes seem as though nature has decided that succeeding generations must rediscover for themselves what elders already know. This is probably because people need to feel that they are self-sufficient. At several stages, children become fiercely resistant to their parents' advice and want to do everything themselves—notably at age two, during the teenage years, and in young adulthood. Understand that if your children sometimes resist your advice, it's not because of what you're saying, but rather it's because it's you who are saying it.

Even so, *how* you're saying it may be contributing to the problem. Yet there is a way to deliver your opinions so they get through. First, choose the right time and the right place—preferably, as I've said, during a prearranged meeting in a pleasant, stress-free setting such as a quiet restaurant or during a stroll along a beach or a country lane. Whenever possible, have these meetings in person rather than over the telephone. Penciling in family members on your calendar and arranging for a place to get together may seem artificial, and I certainly don't mean to rule out the effectiveness of spontaneous heart-to-heart talks, but what I'm trying to help you avoid is falling into the pattern of giving advice in the heat of a disagreement. When that happens, the advice, no matter how valid, is almost always disregarded. And you're most likely to fall into this trap if you let frustrations fester rather than getting your feelings out in the open.

When you do communicate your feelings, however, don't issue orders. Young adults are particularly recalcitrant in the face of being told what to do, and you're better off having a two-way conversation. A simple trick for achieving this is to steer clear of sentences that begin with "You," since they almost always end up sounding one-sided and overly critical. Here's an example of the wrong approach:

> The scene is the kitchen table during a hurried weekday breakfast.
> MOTHER: "You always seem to date men who have no ambition, and Jason is a perfect example. Why would you want to get serious about someone who still hasn't declared a major in his senior year and spends all summer driving around the country in a VW bus that's older than he is instead of holding down a job?"
> DAUGHTER: "Just because *you* married a CPA doesn't mean *I* have to find someone who will bore me to death. Look, I love Daddy, but I have no intention of marrying someone like him. There's got to be more to life than commuting to and from the same office every day for thirty years with two weeks off in August to go to the exact same beach house on the Jersey shore. Give me a break!"

Now everyone is angry and upset, and feeling guilty besides, since no one really wants to hurl invectives at people they love. Worse yet, the daughter has dug in her heels in self-defense so that even if she herself was having second thoughts about Jason, she's now determined to continue the relationship just to show her mother who's calling the shots. Here's a better approach, avoiding the "you" sentences:

> The scene is a restaurant during a relaxed Sunday brunch.
>
> MOTHER: "I understand Jason is trying to make up his mind about what he wants to major in. It must be difficult to make a choice when you're good at so many different things. Maybe he'll have some time to think while he's driving back to school."
>
> DAUGHTER: "Well, I guess you're right about that. I think what's worrying him most is that he's such a talented artist, but he doesn't want to starve to death painting in a garret. And writing poetry isn't exactly going to pay the rent, either. He was thinking of commercial art or journalism, but then he said he'd almost rather do something totally different, like go to law school, and then he could write and paint the way he wants to."
>
> MOTHER: "That's an interesting idea. I actually didn't know he had given this so much thought. I had kind of thought he was a drifter, but I see that I was wrong."
>
> DAUGHTER: "Well, not entirely wrong. I'll admit that it bothers me that he has taken this long to get his act together."
>
> MOTHER: "Really? I never knew that. Maybe we could all get together and talk—you know, brainstorm. Daddy's our resident financial expert. Maybe he could give us some nuts-and-bolts advice about career choices and so on. Ar-

tistic people usually have trouble focusing on the money part."

DAUGHTER: "That'd be great! See, I'm getting really serious about Jason—well, let's be honest, I love him. And of course, I don't expect him to be the only breadwinner. I'm more than willing to work. That's why I'm getting my teaching certificate, after all. But then there might be kids, and all that responsibility. You were a working mother, so you know how that is! Sure, let's all get together. I'd feel a lot better with a little guidance from you guys."

If this last exchange sounds too good to be true, rest assured that it is based on an actual mother/daughter conversation—and that a meeting later on including "Jason" really did result in opening up the lines of communication among all involved. When you avoid blaming and bossing, and treat young people with respect, you will find that they not only stop resisting your help, but are in fact hungry for it.

Include the In-Law-To-Be in Family Rituals and Traditions

Certainly, however, not every interchange with your grown children and their potential spouses has to be a soul-searching session. Now is also the time to learn to enjoy one another. You want your future in-laws to feel comfortable in your family, to understand whatever traditions you have, and to take pleasure in your company. Is Sunday dinner a ritual at your house? Then make a place at the table for the prospective family members as often as all of your schedules permit. Similarly,

whenever possible, include the fiancé(e)s in holiday celebrations, at birthday parties, on outings to football
games, the theater, fishing trips—whatever you all do
together. True, if the kids are away at college, you will
be limited to vacation times and have to share even those
with the intendeds' own families, and possibly stepfamilies. But lobby for as much time as you can get.

By the way, if the prospective bride or groom stays
overnight at your house, I think it's absolutely up to you
whether you let the person share your child's room.
Given the times, the two of them are almost certainly
sexually active, and I hope you have educated them long
before this about safe sex, but I believe you still have the
right to ask the spouse-to-be to sleep on the couch if you
feel strongly about it—or if his or her parents do. The
choice is yours, and if you state your house rules pleas-
antly but firmly, you'll remain in control of the situation.

Establish a One-on-One Relationship with the Person

While family gatherings and celebrations are fun and
promote a sense of belonging to the clan, you would also
do well to make every effort to fit in some private "quality time" with your prospective daughter- or son-in-law.
In-law relationships have traditionally been maligned in
this country—mother-in-law jokes in particular are legion—but there is really no reason that you can't develop
a special and profound bond with the person your child
loves enough to marry and, more important, the person
who will be the mother or father of your grandchildren.
After all, human beings have an infinite capacity for love,
and you are simply adding a new person to the roster of
people you cherish and who feel the same about you.

However, you can't rush this process, and shouldn't

make the mistake of seeing this person as another one of your own children. Your child's intended has a mother and a father (and possibly various stepparents) and doesn't need you in that role. In fact, you'll probably create a good deal of tension if you expect the person to call you "Mom" or "Dad." Then again, what should this newly beloved call you? "Mrs. Doe?" Too formal. "Jane"? Too informal. A lot of people, to tell the truth, just kind of avoid addressing in-laws at all until the first grandchild is born, at which point everyone breathes a sigh of relief because now you have a real title that everyone can use: Grandma or Grandpa—or Nana Rose or Granddaddy or whatever your family invents when the time comes.

Yet no matter how you finesse the problem of what to call each other, you can still share some lovely times. "I had three sons," says one woman, "so when my oldest boy got engaged, I was thrilled to have a girl in the family. But then I got nervous. Did we have anything in common? Would she think it was corny if I wanted to give her my piecrust recipe? Did she like to go shopping? She's a bookworm and doesn't wear any makeup—not that she needs any. She's so pretty. But I mean, she's the natural type, into the environment, and she's a vegetarian. I just couldn't figure out how to connect with her. So I got up my nerve and asked her about her vegetarian diet, and she was really excited. She explained all the benefits, and then she offered to take me to a food co-op where they have whole grains and tofu and kelp and organic fruits and vegetables. We had the best time and then we cooked dinner together, with her teaching me, and the meal was fantastic.

"But guess what we had for dessert: my apple pie. I

showed her how to make a lattice crust—a dying art which I learned from my grandmother. This may not sound like much, but we were laughing and talking and I said I could just picture her passing on the tradition and teaching her children the lattice-crust secret, and she said, 'Oh no, it skips a generation. The grandmother has to do the honors.' And then we both got teary-eyed and my husband and son came in from the back porch and they were shaking their heads, and saying, 'Women!' But they were smiling. You could tell they were pleased we were getting along. My son, especially, looked so relieved!"

Actually, this woman has hit on a very important point. Scientists in a variety of disciplines, from sociology to psychology, have indeed shown that women are innate masters of interpersonal relationships. Throughout history, they have been the "kin keepers," making sure that family constellations stay connected, and in a meaningful way. I do not, however, feel that men should be let off the hook in this regard. There is nothing gender-based about the ability to bond with other people, and there is certainly nothing inborn about the process of keeping a Christmas card list or jotting birthdays and anniversaries on a calendar. With everything else women have to do today, they should not have the sole responsibility for maintaining family ties.

To be fair, however, the youngest of the current crop of grandfathers—those who came of age during the rebirth of American feminism over the last thirty years—may well be more accustomed to what have been called "role-free" households. They have diapered babies and done their share of housework in two-career marriages, and they bring to grandfatherhood a much greater repertoire of hands-on skills and emotional range than do men who are only a decade or two older. But I maintain that almost all grandfathers privately welcome the phase of life that lets them turn from warriors to wise men. They savor the chance to be with little children and they are relieved to relinquish the role of stern disciplinarian. Who, after all, has ever said, "Just wait until your grandfather comes home"? The point I'm making is that grandmothers can tap into this willingness on the part of men to become more involved with family affairs at this stage, and give the men very specific ways to do that, such as planning outings, choosing gifts, and spending time alone with various family members. Again, the moment to begin this "training" is when your child is engaged, so that when grandchildren come along, a genuine closeness among the members of the middle and elder generations, both men and women, has been firmly established.

And be sure the one-on-one relationships are two-way streets, with each of you benefiting from the other. A prime example of someone who accomplished this is the woman we met earlier who learned how to cook a vegetarian meal from her prospective daughter-in-law even as she taught the young woman her own trademark pie-crust secret. Think how much would have been lost if the older woman had dismissed the vegetarian diet as newfangled and crazy, or if the younger woman had refused to bend a little and include a rich dessert on the evening's menu. As it was, each woman gained something from the other, and their friendship began to ripen. Neither one felt threatened or rejected, and over the years this fact will surely translate into the ability to compromise on child-rearing techniques so that the grandmother can pass on her tried-and-true tips but also appreciate the daughter-in-law's state-of-the-art theories.

Get to Know the "Other Grandparents"

Still, as we have noted earlier, your relationship with your child's spouse does not exist in a vacuum. You can bake pies together until kingdom come, but unless you also establish at least a cordial if not an intimate bond with the "other grandparents," you're courting trouble. Yet I recognize that the process of becoming "family" may well be a true challenge. If you already know and like the other side of the family, and if your socioeconomic and religious backgrounds are similar, you're probably more the exception than the rule these days. Even so, learning to understand different ethnic, religious, and regional mores is easy compared to negotiating a peace treaty with people who clearly don't want their child to marry your child in the first place. Rarely these days is this attitude a function of the classic Montague/Capulet family feud that drove Romeo and Juliet to take matters into their own hands with tragic consequences. Far more often, the other family thinks *no one* is really good enough for their precious offspring. This opinion, whether expressed overtly or covertly, can elicit sheer fury in you, since you see it as an affront to your parenting skills, your family, and *your* precious offspring.

"They think they're such big shots," said one woman. "Their son went to prep school and an Ivy League college, and our daughter went to a state school. She worked her way through and she's still paying off student loans because we have three other kids in school. Okay, fine, we're not rich. My husband has a landscaping business and I work part-time at the library. But we live within our means and we're very happy. However, my daughter's fiancé's family thinks we're not in their league. They don't come right out and say it, but the mother, especially, looks down her nose at us. I feel so uncomfortable. And so *mad*! My daughter was brought up with good values, she was an A student and I personally think this boy should be so lucky. Money isn't everything!"

A situation like this is sticky for sure. The best you can do is to hold on to your own values and treat your future child-in-law well. This will surely have a positive effect on the other parents. Still, in particularly stubborn cases, you may not fully succeed in winning people over until the grandchildren are born. Yet if you have at least avoided outright hostility until then, chances are that the birth of a baby who is the living embodiment of your collective heritage will soften the hardest of hearts. Beyond that, the child-in-law who has contributed to the miracle will take on a whole new status in the eyes of people who once didn't "approve" of him or her.

When Your Daughter or Daughter-in-Law Is Pregnant

In fact, the process of softening hard hearts and bonding as an extended family in a new and better way can start during the pregnancy, since everyone knows that the sense of awe, wonder, and humility surrounding the incipient advent of a new human being is virtually universal. That's why I strongly recommend that all of the adults stay very much connected at this special time.

I know that many families live miles apart, but phys-

ical distance does not have to mean emotional distance—
certainly not in an electronic era when phones and
modems and faxes and video cameras combine with traditional ways to stay in touch such as letters and photographs. If you are not just over the river and through
the woods, begin right now to establish regular contact
so that you'll be in good shape for the challenge of long-
distance grandparenting when the baby arrives. Whether
you are in the neighborhood or not, you can be a vital
and welcome part of your grown children's lives as they
prepare for parenthood. Just as you learned to hold successful family councils during the time when your children were engaged, you should now confer and reach a
common ground on the new issues that will arise as your
children become parents and you become grandparents.
The task is certainly more complicated if you don't live
near one another, but make every effort to place conference calls and visit as often as possible during this important stage.

At the beginning of the pregnancy, you might want to
deal with such relatively safe topics as how much time
you will have for your grandchild, how much time you
hope to have alone with your grandchild, how much you
will or won't be available for baby-sitting given your
work schedule and proximity to the new parents, and
whether dropping in will be acceptable to the parents or
whether they would rather have you call first. And see if
you can sort out some kind of a holiday get-together
schedule that seems fair to both sets of grandparents, and
stepparents as well. This may take some negotiating, but
you might as well start now and not wait until the baby
is three months old when Thanksgiving and Christmas
are around the corner.

This is also the time to discuss more sensitive subjects such as whether there will be a christening or a bris, particularly in interfaith households. You saw this coming, of course, but very often young marrieds don't do much about religion until parenthood is on the horizon, and then the issue suddenly becomes quite volatile. You may have to enlist the aid of good friends, or experts such as one or more of the families' clergymen, or even a trained mediator to settle these problems.

Also, be sure to cover the topic of child-rearing philosophies. Yes, you have successfully reared a family, but you would do well to read the same books your children are reading so that you will be abreast of today's trends. You don't have to agree with everything, but at least you'll be prepared. As one woman told me, "My grandson is two months old, and my daughter and I have been having a battle royal over the baby's sleeping position. She says the newest thing is that babies who sleep on their stomachs are more prone to crib death. Some study in France supposedly proved this. But then there is the time-honored notion that if a baby sleeps on his back, he could spit up and choke to death. My daughter says her pediatrician says that theory is an old wives' tale. And I say that she and her brother slept on their stomachs and lived to tell about it. My husband heard us going at it the other day and he said, 'Why don't you just put the kid in the car seat and let him sleep sitting up?' At least he broke the tension and we could all laugh at ourselves."

This is a perfect example of a no-win situation, and the grandfather was a real savior when he made the women see the humor involved. Obviously, the new mother, like most new mothers, is both conscientious and terrified, and if she has heard that sleeping positions are a matter of life or death, it's no wonder she's nervous. In a case like this, I don't think a grandmother helps much by pushing her own theories. She'll only make an already shaky new mother even more confused, and there's no real proof of who's right. For that matter, there's no real proof about a lot of child-rearing theories. I gulped when I saw my own daughter mixing my infant grandson's formula with plain tap water. I was sure she should boil the water first. I put my two cents' worth in, but she said she was following her pediatrician's advice. It wasn't easy to keep quiet after that, but I didn't argue. Justin, the grandchild who was given the bottle with tap water, is now a healthy and strapping eight-year-old, so I've learned my lesson.

Of course, your children are not the only ones involved in bringing up baby. You may find you have differences of opinion with the "other grandparents" as well. But bear in mind that if children have lots of people who love them and care about them, it doesn't matter if there are variations in how those people live. However, do talk to your children and with the other grandparents about values, rules and regulations, and standards under which the children are to be raised. It's important that these be generally consistent between parents and grandparents. But healthy diversity must be honored and respected by all family members. What you all have in common is your love for the child. So don't be concerned if people differ in attitudes, ways, language, and behaviors, as long as the love and values and commitment are similar. For example, perhaps the parents like to have the children eat first and go to bed so the adults can have some private time. In contrast, one set of grandparents may have a big, noisy brood that eats together family-style with relaxed standards, while the other set of grandparents places a high value on formal table manners. There's nothing really wrong with this situation. The children only stand to be enriched by these three variations on a theme, each of which is acceptable and within the range of normal.

An important caveat, however: Tolerance is one thing, but if there is serious pathology or substance abuse in any branch of the family, you are doing no one a favor to cover this up or ignore it in order to save face or just because you hope the problems will go away. All of the current literature on adult children of dysfunctional families points to the fact that the damage done by pretending all's well when it's not is disastrous to youngsters. Yes, it takes tremendous courage to confront people, but you can learn to do it. Consult the appendix at the end of this book for support groups and literature to help you with this challenging but crucial task.

A Grandchild Is Born

So you've navigated the early months of the pregnancy, and now the birth is imminent. Don't miss the moment. Younger grandparents, the "boomers" who pioneered the natural childbirth movement over the last twenty-five years, know firsthand the immeasurable joy that can be shared when fathers act as labor coaches and attend the births of their children. As these same people move up a notch to grandparenthood, they are taking the idea to its natural conclusion, with grandparents going to childbirth classes and attending births along with fathers. Actually, this is really a return to the scenario in the days when women gave birth at home and family members acted as midwives. I don't wish to overromanticize that period, when the rate of death in childbirth was alarmingly high due to complications and childbed fever. But the emotional aspect of a family birth, whether at home or in the hospital or a birthing center, is certainly a plus, and I am firmly in favor of reinstituting it. Of course, even in the past, men were not often included in the birthing process, but today's fathers already know how profound the experience of attending births can be, and today's mothers are much less reticent about sharing the experience with all family members.

I recommend that you make every effort to attend the birth, even if traveling causes some financial strain. I don't mean that you can't bond with your grandchild if you miss the birth. Of course you can, and people have been doing that for years. But I can't emphasize enough the importance of being there when your grandchild comes into the world. I guarantee that you will find yourself overcome by the powerful experience of being present at the creation. I speak from personal experience. My wife and I attended the births of our grandchildren. The glow is with me still. At one point in my medical career, I delivered lots of babies, and every baby I helped to bring into the world was a fresh miracle for me. Yet nothing can compare with the feeling of watching one's own progeny, a generation removed, come into the world via a beloved daughter or daughter-in-law. I had been studying grandparenting for years before my first grandchild was born, but it was at that moment, when the baby emerged, that I knew the urge to grandparent is in our bones and all I had been writing about was true. As I took my turn to hold the child, a thought popped into my head that gave clear meaning and cohesiveness to all of my research into the vital connection between grandparents and grandchildren: "This is what a long life is for."

The First Three Months

The moment of birth, then, is a spiritual pinnacle. Yet for everyone concered, the day-to-day reality of life with a newborn is considerably less glorious. You've been there, so you know. Do absolutely everything you can to relieve the new parents and help them get through this highly stressful period. One grandmother told me: "Suzanne had a fairly easy labor, but the baby was born jaundiced and Suzanne was also having trouble getting him started at the breast. The jaundice was really nothing to be worried about, but she was in a panic. These days they send new mothers home before the milk even comes in, and Suzanne was just so exhausted and scared. The La Leche people were telling her that if she so much as gave the kid one bottle, it was all over for breast-feeding, and the doctor was telling her the bilirubin count was bad and the baby needed a bottle. In the meantime, the baby wouldn't suckle, and Suzanne called me and started sobbing and saying, 'This is supposed to be natural! What's wrong with me?' "

This new grandmother, who lived and worked in another city and had just returned home after attending the birth, decided she was needed on the home front. She called in sick at work, hopped a plane, and was at her daughter's doorstep within hours. She convinced Suzanne to "cheat" and give the baby a bottle. Suzanne slept for the first time in days and so did the baby. The next morning, right on schedule, Suzanne's milk came in and the baby got the hang of suckling with a little cheek nudging from Grandma.

"I stayed a whole week," this woman said. "I wish I could have stayed longer, but I had used up my sick days and my vacation days. Still, a week helped a lot. At least Suzanne got some sleep, and the baby's jaundice all but disappeared. I did what I could."

Indeed, she did. And truly, no matter how scattered our families are today, every bit of input we can give one another is worth the time, effort, and money. We are, after all, forging new ways to be families. We are finding the good that has come out of the last three decades of upheaval, and we are putting the pieces back together in unforeseen and perhaps better ways. As the newly anointed elders of the tribe, the grandparents of the '90s are at the heart of this auspicious healing process. Because you belong to a new generation of grandparents with no role precedents, you are struggling to find a balance between love, work, and play. The rewards will be more than worth the effort—for you and for your families as well.

Let's continue the journey with a look at what nature has in store for you—in mind, body, and spirit.

2

It's All in Your Mind!

Simply by virtue of your longevity, you are a treasure trove of knowledge and the wisdom that is born of experience. You have survived your own childhood, adolescence, and parenting years and guided your children through life's stages as well. You've seen so much and learned so much about human nature that you have the power to prepare your grandchildren for the future. And although they may be resisting their own parents' attempts to prevent them from letting the downside of history repeat itself, because of the vital connection the children really will listen to you and take you seriously. What is so wonderful is that as you teach your grandchildren the lessons of life, even your mistakes be-

*come valuable. Think of this as a time to rectify past
errors in judgment and behavior as you pass on what
you have learned to the most willing and receptive of
pupils, your grandchildren. Your memories, your tales of
times past, and your seasoned view of the world are all
priceless gifts which you alone can offer to your grandchildren.*

My years of studying grandparenting have led me to
create a list of ten very special ways to help you bestow
those gifts. By doing so, you will be sharing the riches of
your mind and heart in order that the children may carry
forward not merely your genetic legacy but also the essence of the unique individual you have become. After
all, you have not only weathered the storms of life but
have been bolstered by the bright interludes that replen-
ish the soul, and the sum of your experience is like no
other on this earth. What is more, you are a member of
a new generation of grandparents—a group that has not
only all the instincts and resources that elders have always possessed, but also the advantages of good health
and the promise of longevity. Your advanced age is an
asset, not a liability. The years that you have ahead of
you should be a time of celebration and affirmation, not
one of waning powers and physical decline. Yours is the
first generation of grandparents in history which can collectively look forward to these bonus decades—twenty
or more extra years in which the soul can ripen to the
fullest. Yes, the physical signs of aging are inevitable to
one extent or another, but even these will be far less
debilitating if you refuse to believe that you are a person

past your prime. You are not someone whose powers are spent. You are not ready to be put out to pasture. On the contrary, you have been given extra years in which to be eminently useful. This is your finest hour—a time to teach and a time to learn.

To understand that, however, you must resist the myriad negative messages which our culture sends out about the elderly. Only then can your grandparenting years become the period of spiritual growth and untold pleasure they were meant to be. And when you see yourself as a valuable person who has achieved a well-deserved place at the head of the family, everyone will gain from your strength. Still, I recognize that in this country the stereotype of the doddering, demented, meddlesome old person is pervasive and difficult to ignore. A friend of mine told me about the day she went into a Hallmark store to buy a thirtieth-birthday card for a co-worker. She found a large display devoted to the theme of "Over the Hill," which included items for people turning thirty. There were cards, plates, napkins, balloons, buttons, yard signs, and streamers as well as coffee mugs, T-shirts, and baseball caps with slogans and verses about the inevitability of gray hair, wrinkles, aches and pains, and the loss of everything from good eyesight to an operating sex drive.

I was stunned by this. Among the people I know who are thirtysomething and well beyond, a good number are vibrantly alive. Yet as I reflected, I realized that there are others who really *do* seem old. What, I wondered, makes some people seem more elderly than others? Could it be gray hair? No, there's Joe, a sixty-seven-year-old restaurant owner, who has absolutely white hair and is one of the most vital people I know. Well then, wrinkles. No, there's Kelly, fifty-two; an avid tennis player, who's always out in the sun, but her leathery, etched face is radiant and alive. Neither of these people seems old to me. So if looks don't count for everything, what does? The answer is vitality, which is a combination of energy, spirit, and an optimistic attitude.

Optimism, in fact, is an especially important part of the recipe for vitality, according to recent research done at the University of Michigan in the Department of Psychology. Christopher Peterson, principal researcher and coauthor of *Health and Optimism,* says: "Our data show that people who stay young at heart are very focused on the future, in a hopeful way, but not with unrealistic expectations. They have what we call 'reality-based expectations.' That is, they recognize their potential as well as their limitations, and they keep striving for new goals. They go after what they want."

However, Peterson stresses that the brand of optimism which translates into being young-thinking should not be confused with immaturity. "I am not talking about childish people," he maintains. "Childish people have foolish expectations. The noted psychologist Erik Erikson talks about people who have not developed past a certain stage. Usually, they feel they are entitled to be taken care of. They are not vital, not future-oriented. They are stuck in the past." On the other hand, Peterson's subjects who look to the future eagerly are the ones who remain psychologically vital.

Of course, a positive outlook cannot prevent the march of time altogether. But Doreen Gluckin, M.D., author of *The Body at Thirty,* puts a positive spin on that fact, saying: "We all change, each one of us a little differently. Big deal. What *is* a big deal is how we respond to inevitable changes. Change is not a sentence; it's an opportunity. Every time we change, we become different, brand-new people able to take on life from fresh perspectives and with new abilities. The process of change stimulates us away from shallow physical myopia, and toward a richer, fuller awareness of ourselves and our lives, wants, needs, capabilities, and limitations."

I heartily agree. If you look, there are vital people all around you who see life as an ongoing adventure. There are grandparents going to college. There are people long past midlife who are working out regularly, starting their own businesses, maintaining old relationships, and forming new friendships among young and old alike.

Thinking about all of that, I asked my friend what she had done about buying a card for her co-worker. My friend smiled and said she had left the card store empty-handed and gone to a florist. She bought her colleague an azalea bush, a perennial which bursts forth each year with brilliant fuchsia blossoms. And she enclosed a card on which she had written, "Happy thirtieth birthday to someone who has flowered over the years. May you continue to bloom anew with each coming season of your life."

Whatever your age, I sincerely wish the same to you, not just for your sake, but for your grandchildren's as well. After all, only if you maintain your commitment to a lifetime of vitality and spiritual growth will you be prepared to put "grandparent power" to work by performing the ten vital roles that follow.

1. LIVING ANCESTOR AND FAMILY HISTORIAN

Sometime between a child's second and third birthday, he or she is sure to ask, "Where did I come from?" Traditionally, this is the time when parents swallow hard and embark on some version of "the facts of life." I wonder, though, whether little children are not asking a more profound question than adults realize. Is a scientific explanation of conception, pregnancy, and birth really all that a child wants? I believe that he is also curious on a much grander scale about his lineage, his ancestry, the genetic and cultural heritages which make him unique.

This, of course, is where you come in. As a living link to your family's past, you can act as the family historian for your grandchild. In many cultures throughout history, grandparents were the oral historians for the group as a whole and the family in particular, and that role is still extremely valuable today. This fact has led Dr. David Gutmann, a noted psychologist, to describe grandparents as "the wardens of culture."

True, we live in an electronic era, the so-called information explosion, but don't think for a minute that this makes your homespun yarns obsolete. In fact, why not take advantage of current technology and tape-record or videotape your remembrances of things past? Various scholars have been conducting oral history projects in recent years, recognizing that there is a great storehouse of information and opinions locked in the minds of the elder generation. So you might as well do your part toward preserving the lessons of yesterday for the citizens of tomorrow by creating a family archive.

Many of the children I've interviewed have told me they love the fact that their grandparents lived in another time. Piggybacking on your experience, your grandchildren can time-travel from the present to the past. By spinning stories, you can provide your grandchildren with firsthand accounts of other worlds and famous places and events, transporting them beyond their immediate experience. One young man, now a sophomore in college, tells of visiting his eighty-nine-year-old grandmother while en route to school after summer vacation:

"It was awesome! Sure, I had always thought she was really cool, and we got along great from the time I was a little boy, but this was the first time I was alone at her house, without my parents and my sisters. She lives pretty far away, and we usually only saw her at Christmas. Anyway, on this visit I had her all to myself and I had plenty of time before the dorms would be open, so I wasn't in any rush to get back on the road. She has a really neat little house on a lake in Wisconsin, and she is totally healthy, lives all by herself, and rakes the lawn and everything. She has a lot of friends, but I could tell she was really glad to see me. She always says she never had a son so that makes me extra special to her. I stayed a couple of weeks, and we cooked and listened to music, and mostly we talked.

"Well, *she* talked. Just think, she's been alive since right after the turn of the century! All that stuff I read about in school, well, she was actually *there*. She was telling me about the Model T Ford, and the radio, and Lindbergh. She said that when she was seventeen she was already a teacher in a one-room schoolhouse and she rode a horse there and back! Then she was telling me about the Roaring Twenties and she showed me pictures of her and my grandpa. He died when I was a baby, so I don't remember him, but she told me all about him, how he played a cornet in a band and liked to play pool. Later he became a dentist. She says I favor him. Anyway, Grandma just kept talking and I kept asking questions and it was the best. As I said, we were always close even though we lived far apart, but now I really feel connected to her. I wish she'd live forever. Maybe she will. She gets around great and she still has all of her teeth!"

Like this grandmother, you can provide your own grandchildren with a link to their personal pasts through descriptions of the quirks and heroic acts of yourself and of relatives long dead. You can act as the family archivist, chronicling the history of your entire family. When you provide your grandchildren with a sense of history and family roots by playing out the role of living ancestor and historian, when you pass on family ways, rites, and rituals, you teach your grandchildren to think in terms of "we" as well as "I." An individual child who thinks in terms of "we" feels part of a big historical continuum, and that makes the child feel secure and rooted not only to the past, but to the present and the future as well.

2. ROLE MODEL

You are, of course, not just a chronicler of the past, but a person still very much alive in the present. As such, you represent a powerful role model for your grandchildren. You provide them with a model for many aspects of life, but one of the most important object lessons you provide is how to age. The young man we just met who visited his eighty-nine-year-old grandmother was inspired by her vitality and good health, her active lifestyle and her vibrant sense of living each moment fully. This made a profound impression on him which will surely endure and will influence the way he perceives other elderly people, as well as the way he anticipates his own aging in years to come. Without question, this boy's wish that his grandmother could "live forever" will come true, not in the physical sense, but in the way she has illuminated him with her spirit, which he will in turn pass on to succeeding generations, changed only by the addition of his own richness. Yet even grandparents who for one reason or another are not as fit as this boy's grandmother can exert potent, positive influences on their grandchildren.

"My grandfather had Parkinson's disease," recalls a woman now in her twenties. "Toward the end, he was in a wheelchair and his speech was slurred. But he was sharp as a tack, and he never lost his sense of humor. He loved to have me sit and listen to his jokes and stories, and I could understand him better than anyone. Also, I'd play the piano for him, and he just adored that. He would get a kind of dreamy look in his eyes. I admired his courage so much. I miss him right this minute just as much as I did the day he died ten years ago. I'll never forget him, and I hope I'll always be as funny and brave as he was."

As this case illustrates, the stronger and more vital the connection between the grandparent and the grandchild, the more immune the child becomes to socially induced stereotypes of aging. If your grandchild has a positive connection with you, it is likely that the youngster will have a positive perception of the elderly in general, despite the mistreatment that many seniors in our society receive.

In most cases, your grandchild will carry this positive perception into adulthood. I've met a number of people who have told me that they chose the same career as their grandparents because they were very close to them. I have also met many devoted grandchildren, grown into adulthood, who were willing to take their aging grandparents into their homes to nurse them, even before their own parents would do so. And like the woman whose beloved grandfather died of Parkinson's disease, these adult grandchildren see their grandparents as role models for a positive example of how to deal with death. In fact, even young children can benefit in this way. While there is often reluctance on the part of family members to expose children to a dying grandparent, children over the age of five are usually equipped to handle saying goodbye to a grandparent.

> "I was eight years old and my brother, Scott, was six when our grandmother died," recalls a woman who is now the mother of two school-age children. "Nana had always lived with us. She had a little apartment over the garage, but she was in and out of our house all the time, cooking, eating with us, helping us with our homework, or just sitting there knitting and smiling at us. She'd say, 'I don't want to miss any of your little growin'.'
>
> "She wasn't all that old, just in her late sixties. But she had a stroke, and she never fully recov-

ered. She was back and forth to the doctor and
the hospital, and I remember my parents whispering about her. Scott and I would put a glass
against the bedroom wall so we could hear them
in the living room on the other side. Sometimes
they'd say Nana was 'failing.' Other times they'd
say she had 'rallied.' I looked that up in the
dictionary and there were so many definitions,
but then I found one that said 'a sharp improvement in vigor, health or spirits.' I told Scott. But
we knew. We knew the improvement wasn't going to last. One time, I got up the nerve to ask
my mother if Nana was going to die, and my
mother said everybody dies and just left it at that.
Then I asked Nana what was going to happen to
her, and it was hard for her to speak clearly at
that point, but she said very carefully, 'When my
time comes, I'll be ready.' I gave her a big hug
and told her I would always love her.

"Not long after that, Nana had another stroke,
in her own bed. We had moved her out of her
apartment into Scott's room, and Scott was sharing my room, so we were right down the hall.
There wasn't time to get Nana to the hospital.
Our parents didn't know what to do. They were
on the phone to the doctor, and they were just
ignoring Scott and me. So we walked into Nana's
room quietly and we each took one of her hands.
We brushed the hair off her forehead and kissed
her. Our parents came in then and stood beside
us. Scotty started to sing real softly, 'Jesus loves
me, this I know, 'cause the Bible tells me so,' and
we all joined in. Nana kind of flickered a smile,

her eyes lit up, and then the light went out. I felt
her hand change: the life went out of it. I will
always have that moment. I got to say good-bye.
No one can take that away from me. And I think
her spirit is living still. She sees my children, her
great-grandchildren, and she's not missing any of
their little growin'."

Many other people have told me similar stories. When
I asked an eleven-year-old girl whose grandmother had
died two years earlier to describe her, she said: "She's
still alive for me. She died in the hospital, and I went to
the funeral, but she's still so real to me. If I close my
eyes, I can smell her rosewater-and-glycerin hand cream.
I remember how she held me in her lap. She was very
soft. I used to kind of melt into her. Now it's like I expect
her to be there when I get home from school. I know she
won't be there, of course, but she's not dead for me. I
feel her when I want to. I just close my eyes, and she's
there."

For a lot of children, a departed grandparent stays forever in the heart and mind in a state of suspended ani-
mation. These children don't really imagine aging and
death as something to be feared. But that doesn't mean
that the death of a grandparent is easy for children. Often when parents are grieving over the loss of a parent,
they fail to recognize the grieving that their own children
are going through as well. But when a young grandchild
experiences the death of a beloved grandparent, it is a
powerful event. As one young woman told me, "When
my grandmother died, my parents had a public mourning
with our big family, but mine was a private mourning,
because no one paid attention to what the children were

feeling. None of the grown-ups had any idea that my grandmother was the center of the magic in my life. She was my partner in a gracious and happy other reality."

This statement is a poignant example of how the links between the generations can be oddly disconnected even in families that have not been rent asunder by divorce. You can help to remedy that situation in your own family by providing examples of how to set a positive tone for the family. When your grandchild sees that you and her parents get along and are happy together, the child is likely to develop a positive image of parents and grandparents. Children who live in families where the older generations get along well learn that these generations are vital parts of a happy, harmonious family. And being the copycats that they are, these children will bring that piece of wisdom to their families when they become parents.

It's important to remember, however, that this copycat aspect of role modeling can work negatively too, especially in cases when families are feuding. It can even lead to grandparents being deprived of access to their grandchildren. Children often hold an unexpressed grudge against parents who feud with grandparents. Children resent the parents' interference in what is usually a happy and carefree relationship. The anger goes even deeper when the parents won't let the youngsters see their grandparents at all. Children become especially unsettled and frightened and mistrustful of their parents if they see them reject their grandparents, because they fear that parents might reject or even abandon them someday as well. Children have also told me that they are frightened by the idea that they might someday reject their own parents. After all, when parents mistreat grandparents and shut them out of the lives of their family, they are teaching their children that abandonment is a way of dealing with intergenerational conflicts and problems.

This situation is so dangerous that it warrants a warning: Parents who shun grandparents and do not strive to find better solutions to their problems should not be surprised if they are later treated the same way by their own children. As one ten-year-old whose family was involved in a drawn-out visitation case told me, "If I don't get along with my own parents someday, if they don't do what I like, I just won't talk to them anymore or let them see my children." Remember, children live according to the expression "Monkey see, monkey do." This is why I want to stress once again that you need to do your part from the very beginning to nurture your relationship with the middle generation as a preventive measure against a painful rupture later on. Here again, you can be the one who sets the right example of tolerance and reasonable compromise for both the middle and the youngest generations to follow.

3. TEACHER

Yet if you influence your family by example, you can also shape your grandchildren in a more conscious and active way. The role of teacher is one of the most important that you have as a grandparent. Sadly, it is also perhaps the most underrated in the current social climate. This is particularly lamentable given the fact that grandparents were the first professors, and their knowledge and wisdom was held in great esteem throughout most of history. What you must remember is that even today it is your inalienable right to teach your grandchildren what you know, whether or not people think you are old-fashioned because what you teach may not be in vogue. You have the right and the responsibility to run your own classroom about life, to develop your own curriculum. Whatever your specialties may be—baking, whittling, singing, speaking a foreign language, playing chess, gardening, knitting, skiing, swimming, diving, braiding hair—teach them to your grandchildren. In fact, the less up-to-date your skill, the more important it is for you to pass it on. Did your own grandmother teach you how to tat or cross-stitch? Then don't let the lessons die with you. And remember there are no books, no lesson plans, and no videotapes that will ever be as effective as personal coaching, particularly when teacher and student are linked by love.

As one young woman told me, "I took ballet lessons when I was a little girl, and my grandmother was the one who chauffeured me. She had been a dancer in her youth in Russia, and before my first lesson, when I was eight years old, she taught me how to do the right hairstyle, with looped braids caught up in colored ribbons. I practiced and practiced until I got it smooth and perfect. My teacher was so impressed. Then, over the years, my grandmother taught me how to make a bun and a twist, the more grown-up styles. She showed me pictures of herself as a girl with exactly the same hairstyles. I loved that, especially since I look so much like her."

Like this granddaughter, or a grandson I know whose grandfather taught him how to talk to farm animals, your grandchild is primed to benefit from what you teach. The unique brand of information that you impart to your grandchildren adds diversity to their storehouse of knowledge and contributes to their uniqueness and individuality—their specialness. It also adds to their ability to think critically about the world and to view life in perspective.

There are no limits to the quantity and quality of the knowledge which you can impart. You enrich your grandchildren with things children learn nowhere else, especially in these times when they get so little undivided attention from other people, and are taught in such a structured and limited way in school. Because your grandchildren usually view their time with you as fun time, and because your emotional attachment has a natural tendency to be so strong, your grandchild learns from you almost unconsciously. As one precocious grandchild said, "It's like osmosis." There is no need for pointers and chalkboards when you are teaching. Your love and dedication make your lessons stick firmly in your grandchild's mind. I know a number of adults who report that what they learned from their grandparents often "stuck" better than what they learned from their parents. This is because children don't feel the need to oppose their grandparents as they do their parents. They accept information from their grandparents much more easily. Take advantage of this situation. You will be passing on what you know to people you will never see. By teaching your grandchildren and influencing the kind of people they become, you will achieve a very real kind of immortality. And all this will benefit your grandchild as well.

Unfortunately, sometimes your own children will worry about what you teach their kids. What you impart may be at odds with what your children want for their children. This can be an especially pressing issue, for example, for new immigrants coming to America who want to discard the old ways and start over in their new country as quickly as possible.

Li, a Chinese grandmother, had lots of problems with her daughter-in-law Ellie because Li wanted to teach her granddaughter Connie, age ten, about her heritage. Connie was fascinated by what her grandmother taught her—family history, special family recipes, the stories behind old family costumes, and memories from Li's childhood. The fireworks started when Li told Connie that it was important to cook well in order to please her husband. When Connie's mother, Ellie, heard that, Connie said, she "had a cow."

Ellie agreed, "My mother-in-law is brainwashing my daughter. She's teaching Connie to be submissive," she told me. "I want her to be a liberated woman, not like the women in the old county who were nothing more than slaves. Li still thinks that pleasing a man's palate is the highest calling in life for a woman."

Li couldn't understand why Ellie was so vehement about her teaching Connie to please a husband. "What's wrong with teaching my Connie to be a wife and mother?" Li lamented. "If Ellie paid more attention to that, my son would be happier."

Since the conflict was not getting resolved, I suggested that everyone sit down and talk things over. Li pointed out to Connie's mother that she wasn't teaching Connie "submissiveness" at all. She only wanted to teach Connie her family history, telling her about her ancestors and giving her a sense of rootedness and continuity. "I am teaching Connie to know me, and to know our ancestors, who are with me every day," Li said. She continued, "And for a woman to take care of a home is not submissiveness, it's working together with the husband for the family. It's being a family."

Together, we decided to allow Connie to judge whether or not she was being "brainwashed" by her grandmother. "I am not being 'brainwashed' by my grandmother at all," Connie told me. "I love most of the stuff she teaches me. Some of the ancestor stuff, well, I don't really understand, but she is very serious about it. She does have old-fashioned ideas, but they're interesting. I love to listen to her. All we're doing is just having fun. Besides, I hate to cook. My husband will have to cook his own food."

If your children are having difficulty with what you are teaching your grandchild, talk this problem over with them. Discuss the issue openly and come to an appropriate compromise. Generational differences in attitudes, values, and outlook are to be expected, especially in a society changing as rapidly as ours. Yet if you use the "family council" technique you learned when your grandchildren's parents were engaged, you'll be able to reach a meeting of minds that will benefit everyone. Here again, the crucial issue is to avoid needlessly alienating the middle generation, since your access to your grandchildren depends on their goodwill.

4. MENTOR

Still another reason to maintain that goodwill is so that you can act as your grandchildren's mentor. This role is different from that of teacher in that you are not simply transmitting skills. You are firing the children's ambition and imagination, giving them a sense of their own worth and promise, tilling their spirit. The word *mentor* is currently defined as "wise and trusted counselor" and it comes to us from Greek mythology. Mentor was Odysseus's trusted counselor, and it was in Mentor's disguise that Athena became the guardian and teacher of Odysseus's son Telemachus in his father's absence.

The importance of the mentor role cannot be overstated. As you know, children spend most of their time in schools, taking tests, getting grades, and learning from a cast of teachers that usually changes from year to year. Occasionally, a child will find a special teacher who will take the child under his or her wing, but most often there is no sense of continuity or permanence in the learning environment. Each fall, a child must prove herself anew, and a youngster can easily begin to wonder, in this highly competitive age, just what is special or valuable about herself. This, needless to say, is risky business, and only a one-on-one relationship with a mentor can ameliorate the problem. In fact, the research of distinguished Harvard University psychiatrist Robert Coles has shown that even children with severe problems such as dysfunctional families, learning disabilities, or physical handicaps can grow up to be whole and happy people if each child has just one person who is rooting for and believes in him. Coles calls these fortunate youngsters "the invulnerables." As we have seen, however, parents are not always in the right emotional position to fulfill the mentor role, since they are directly responsible for the child's welfare and discipline as well as often being consumed by the task of making practical decisions about the child's day-to-day life. But as a grandparent, you have the luxury of being available for the mentor role.

As one young man told me, "I'm dyslexic, and I had to repeat first grade. I thought I was dumb, and I felt so bad in September when all my friends were in second grade and I was with a bunch of babies I didn't even know. My parents and teachers were trying to say all the right things, but my parents were so busy, with both of them working, and my sister and I had to go to an after-school center until six every night.

"Then, at Christmas, my grandma came to visit. She had been a kindergarten teacher herself, and she brought some picture books and had me tell her stories from looking at the books. I didn't have to read any words. I did it all with my imagination. She got really excited, and she wrote the stories down. I did pretty well reading them back to her, because I knew what I had said. That felt so good. She told me a boy with a mind like mine was very special, a genius even. I believed her. And she told me never to forget that she was my biggest booster.

"When I got older, I eventually learned to read, although I still can't spell. I loved science-fiction books. Then my grandmother gave me a computer for my twelfth birthday, with a spell checker, and I wrote a whole novel. I read it the other day and it's really good. Maybe I'll polish it up and get it published. Who cares if I can't spell? Any old machine can do that!"

Like this grandmother, you are in a natural position to play the role of mentor for your grandchildren—and they need you whether they are gifted or average, disabled or fit. None of us is perfect and each of us is special. The combination of talents and abilities your grandchildren have are theirs alone, and you can help them recognize that and inspire them to strive to fulfill their one-of-a-kind potential. The best way to do that is focus on their strengths, not their weaknesses. Deepak Chopra, M.D., author of the best-selling book *Ageless Body, Timeless Mind,* bemoans the fact that Americans seem determined to "fix" what is wrong with their children at the expense of nourishing what is right. "If a child is weak at math, but he's a natural artist, don't get him a math tutor," says Dr. Chopra. "Get him a canvas and some oil paints. Let him be what he was born to be. You have no right to interfere with that." Indeed, accentuating the positive is a special function of grandparents.

In the role of mentor, then, you have the power to spark your grandchildren's imagination, and provide them with inspiration and motivation that will last them a lifetime.

5. STUDENT

Remember that the grandparent/grandchild connection is not a one-way street. Even as you teach and inspire your grandchildren, they can teach and inspire you. Forget that tired old maxim about an old dog not being able to learn new tricks. Let yourself enter the fresh and evolving world of a child. You will absorb information and insights no matter what your age. This doesn't mean you won't have to put forth some effort, however. Just as you lose physical prowess more quickly if you are sedentary than if you are active, you lose mental agility if you stop exercising your mind. You may be a bit rusty, but the desire and ability to learn will resurge with exhilarating force if you will simply open yourself to the possibilities. Let your grandchild take you by the hand and lead you into the future. Computers, modems, fax machines, the rules for playing soccer, new research in science and math—whatever seems intimidating and beyond your grasp can be made comprehensible and fun by the gentlest and most eager of teachers, your grandchild.

"My grandma was terrified of the ATM at the bank,"

says a teenage girl. "She is a smart lady, and she has managed her own money since my grandpa died seven years ago, but you couldn't get her to go near those machines. She wouldn't even apply for a card. She'd stand on long lines, waiting for a teller, just for the simplest transaction. Well, finally one day when she and I had gone shopping, we were having lunch and I said I was out of cash and I asked if she would just come to the machine with me. I was excited because I had gotten my own card only a couple of months before that when I turned eighteen. I work part-time in the drugstore and I love having my own account.

"Anyway, Grandma reluctantly agreed to go to the machine with me. I kind of teased and challenged her and so on, and she started getting into it. Then she saw how simple it was and she was really getting a kick out of it. But her fear was that the machine would make a mistake and take your money or something. She just didn't trust it. I explained the safeguards and said I thought the machine was more reliable than most people I know. That really cracked her up. Well, end of story, she got herself a card, and her first Touch-Tone phone. Now she loves to use the phone to do her banking right from home. She's seventy-four, and she's a real whiz at it. I told my parents we should all chip in and buy her a computer for her seventy-fifth birthday!"

I have heard lots of similar stories from grandparents and grandchildren of varying ages. One of the most touching was that of a grandmother who had been illiterate all her life. Her three-year-old grandson went to a Montessori nursery school where there were special tactile letters of the alphabet made from sandpaper. The children traced the letters with their fingers in order to learn the shapes. On visiting day, this grandmother tried the technique along with her grandson, and reports that "suddenly it began to make sense." Inspired, she enrolled in a literacy tutoring program, and learned to read at last. "Now I read to my grandson and he reads to me," she reports. "Learning to read has changed my life, and I have Johnny to thank for that."

6. NURTURER

And so, to paraphrase the Bible, a little child can lead us. Still, in an era when children grow up too fast on a diet of sex and violence in the media, let us not abrogate our right and responsibility to maintain our position as elders, and to care for our children. They may know many things, but that does not make them wise or mature. So learn from your grandchildren, but do not fail to let them know that you and their parents are still in charge of their upbringing. Far from alienating the children, this firm stance on your part will make them feel safe. In the physical sense, they need adults to provide food and shelter and care when they are ill, but in a more profound way, they need you to give them the values and strengths and beliefs they must have in order to survive in an increasingly complex world. But you know that in your heart. The role of nurturer is, in many ways, among the most basic of those that you play for your grandchild. It stems from your biological and emotional urges to care for your children and grandchildren and their need for you to care for them. Your role as a family nurturer benefits not only your grandchildren but your own children, providing them with a natural safety net. Grandmothers especially are frequently called on to be a mother's personal support system. Child care, nursing, counseling, providing financial and emotional support, and acting as "the family watchdog," as research psychologist Lillian Troll puts it, are just a few of the ways that you succor your family.

And you are not the only who senses that nurturing is a natural role for you. Your grandchildren also intuitively understand that they have been supplied with more adults than just their two parents to care for them. When you act as a backup nurturing system by supporting their parents, you expand your grandchild's life support system and make the child feel secure. Professor Gunhild O. Hagestad, a professor at the College of Human Development of Pennsylvania State University, has described the way in which reliable and trustworthy grandparents act as a deterrent to family disruption and exert a calming influence in often catastrophic situations. She calls grandparents the family's "national guard."

A bit of caution here, however. The nurturing role is not without its pitfalls. Even though you can benefit your grandchild in this role, some grandparents who pursue the nurturing role too enthusiastically may be seen by insecure parents as being overcontrolling or meddlesome. It's often a tough call to make: Is a grandmother who protests when her son takes her three-year-old grandson skiing being overprotective or is her son being irresponsible? Even so, if you do cross the line and become too "meddlesome" for the liking of the parents, your grandchildren will still appreciate the attention. As one child happily told me, "Whenever I'm late, or I hurt myself, or I don't go to the bathroom every day, my grandmother gets very worried."

Of course, the nurturing role of grandparents really comes to the fore when adversity strikes. In divorce cases, for example, the parents may be so consumed with their own pain and legal battles, in addition to their regular responsibilities at work, that they have less time for the children than ever. One teenage boy recalls such a situation: "I felt like I was abandoned in my own home. My father had left to live with his girlfriend, and my mother was a total wreck, always on the phone crying or shouting or talking to her lawyer. I had developed a kind of way of just smiling through everything. I don't think my parents even knew how scared I was. I was ten years old at the time. But it was Grandpa Joe who saved me. He caught on. He knew I was hurting. He started showing up more than usual, and he took me to the ball game with two of my friends, and he had me sleep over a lot. He'd tell stories and make me laugh. He'd say we were the men of the family, and that made me proud.

"Also, Grandma Rose had died two years before, so Grandpa Joe was on his own, and he told me he needed me in his life. That did it. I didn't feel like the one who was all alone. I felt like I had a job to do. My Grandpa Joe needed me and I was going to be his pal.

"Eventually, the divorce thing was final, and my mom settled down. My dad started taking me every other weekend. I got used to it. But it was Grandpa Joe who held me together. Grandpa Joe spent time with my dad, too. That made me feel good. I don't even think my parents know how much Grandpa Joe helped all of us."

This grandfather demonstrates just how effective men can be at nurturing, and as we have noted before, the role becomes much more natural for men when they are grandfathers than it was when they were fathers. Even so, grandmothers are still the ones most likely to be called upon to help, particularly in divorce situations, simply because the divorced custodial mother will most likely turn to her own mother for help and support. The other grandparents should be aware that this is a natural reflex on the part of the mother, and they should persevere in their attempts to nurture not only their grandchildren but both of the parents as well.

With the recent increase in reports of child abuse, another dimension of the grandparental nurturing role has come to light. When grandchildren are being abused, especially by their own parents or stepparents, grandchildren often turn to their grandparents for help. My research has even shown that involved grandmothers are often the first ones to sense that something is wrong. Lately, "Grandparents Raising Grandchildren" organizations have sprouted up around the country in response to family breakdown and the increase in reported child abuse. According to the Census Bureau, there are more than 4 million grandparents now raising their grandchildren. This is no surprise when we consider that currently 22 percent of children are born out of wedlock, one-third of them to teenage mothers. As one grandmother raising her grandchild told me, "When my grandchild is in danger, the buck stops with me. They'll put him in a foster home over my dead body."

7. Genie
Fortunately, however, not all of your roles as a grandparent are quite so demanding as the ones we have looked at thus far. Moving into the realm of unalloyed joy, think about how glorious it is to simply have fun with this special child who loves you as much as you love her. You can act as a magical genie with the power

to grant her wishes. You can lavish her with attention and treats, and revel with her in childhood pleasures. In other words, you have the right to spoil your grandchild. And when you spoil her, you are doing nothing more than expressing the unconditional love and fun of your relationship, rejoicing in one another's existence.

Unfortunately, however, while spoiling your grandchild may be one of the greatest joys of your life, parents don't always appreciate what you're doing. Some parents get jealous of their own children, feeling that you don't—or never did—treat them the same way. Whether or not this condition develops depends on how cooperative or competitive the family is, or on how much fun you were able to have with your own children. For most parents, if you and their children are happy, they are happy too. But if a misunderstanding does exist on the part of your own children, be considerate of their feelings. Sure you can indulge a grandchild according to his own fancy, as long as the grandchild is happy, the activity is not dangerous, and it doesn't bother the parents too much. But if it does bother a parent, look at this as a signal that perhaps your own child needs a bit more of you too.

For example, twelve-year-old Felicia and her grandmother Denise like to go shopping. Felicia's mother, Leslie, feels that Denise is spoiling Felicia, making her feel entitled to expensive designer clothes and ruining her sense of the value of a dollar.

"I can't afford to buy Felicia the kind of clothes my mother lets her have," says Leslie. "I'm a single mother and I want Felicia to have a realistic understanding of our situation. I feel that if she wants something special, she should baby-sit and pay for it herself. But my mother just buys anything for her. My mother is not rich, but my father left her pretty well set, and she has few expenses, so she just spends like crazy on Felicia.

"And it's not just that I don't want Felicia to get the wrong values. It also burns me up because my mother was a total tightwad when I was growing up. I remember in the eighth grade, I was dying for a cashmere sweater set. That was the 'in' thing, to have a pullover and a cardigan, and a string of pearls. I had seen a blue twin set that matched my eyes, and my mother said I didn't need it. She said I had enough hand-me-downs from my cousin Karen."

For her part, Denise told me with a smile that going shopping with Felicia is one of the greatest pleasures in her life.

"Times were harder for me when Leslie was young," says Denise. "My husband was a construction worker, and there would be money in the summer and then everything would dry up as the work slowed down in the winter. Sometimes we were literally living hand-to-mouth. But we saved what we could, and we bought a nice house and over the years, things got better. Now I have my nest egg and my Social Security, and I think I deserve to have a little fun. I'm not getting any younger. So if I want to buy my gorgeous granddaughter a new outfit, what's so terrible?"

Having heard both sides of the story, I suggested to Denise that she take Leslie shopping alone once in a while. This simple solution worked liked magic. The secret here is that no matter how crazy you are about your grandchild, don't forget to treat your own kids as well as you treat your grandchildren once in a while.

8. CRONY

This is not to say, however, that you can't have a relationship with your grandchild which excludes your own children. I believe that one of your most delightful tasks as a grandparent is to be a crony, a pal, a secret conspirator with your grandchild. I'm not suggesting, of course, that you're going to do anything foolish, but only that as an elder who is not responsible for every detail of the child's upbringing, you can afford to indulge in a bit of harmless mischief.

"At my grandma's house, I always got to wear red nail polish," recalls one woman. "She had been a very glamorous woman in her day, and even in her sixties, she was quite stylish. She wore big hats and lots of jewelry and perfume. And she had long red nails. I just adored her. My own mother was much more conservative, and when I begged my mom to let me wear makeup, even just a little blush and lip gloss, she said absolutely not until I was sixteen. I was eleven at the time, and I told my grandmother about this when I was over there one afternoon. She just kind of laughed and said, 'A little nail polish can't hurt.' And she did my nails, a whole manicure with cuticle remover and everything. I could have swooned, I was so excited. And then she let me use some of her perfume. It was very rich-smelling and she kept it in a fancy crystal bottle with a stopper in the shape of an orchid.

"Anyway, I had to take the nail polish off before I went home, but this got to be our ritual, our secret. Every time I went over to Grandma's, I got a manicure and some perfume."

Obviously, the role of crony can be an enormous

amount of fun, but it can also get you into trouble if you're not good at covering your tracks. If you should happen to be found out, you may be seen as someone who is enticing your grandchild to conspire against the parents. One sardonic bit of popular wisdom acknowledges this: "Grandparents and grandchildren get along so well because they both have the same enemies." While there may be some truth to this statement—the obvious unfairness to parents notwithstanding—it takes the conspiratorial role of grandparents far too seriously. Yes, you and your child will often interpret your relationship with your grandchild differently, but the circumstances surrounding these conspiratorial situations are usually harmless and amusing—to everyone except the parents, that is. One young woman told me that her grandfather used to let her drive his truck when she was eight years old, telling her "to keep it our secret." She said her parents "freaked out" when they found out.

Also, don't be surprised if your children envy the comradery that you share with your grandchild. That is natural. But mature parents understand that this conspiratorial behavior is just plain fun, and they look the other way. Unfortunately, however, the natural alliance between grandparents and grandchildren can erupt into a major problem when grandparents and parents are feuding. You don't want the children to end up as pawns in a battle of wills between the elder and middle generations. Be forewarned that if you let that happen, you haven't got a chance of being the winner. So indulge in your little pranks, but never go so far as to undermine the parents' ultimate authority or to risk angering them with an open confrontation. In other words, keep the role of crony in its proper place as a source of great good cheer and companionship with your little co-conspirators.

One last word of caution, however. Be sure you don't spend all of your crony time with only one grandchild. Let's face it: It's human nature to have a favorite among your grandchildren. Whether he's the firstborn or the one that's a lot like you, this special bond is sure to happen. When it does, it's great for the anointed one, and not so great for the others. Remember, no matter how you feel about one child or another, your grandchildren all look up to you. Children suffer when they aren't "picked" by their grandparents, especially in a family with a competitive nature. Chris, age seven, wasn't picked by his grandpa: "He always wants to play ball with my brother because he's better. I get left out. Just because my grandfather was a baseball player."

Favoritism when taken to this extreme can be hurtful to children. Every child is special, and it's especially up to grandparents to make each child feel that way. Spread your love around equally.

9. Wizard

If the role of crony makes you a kind of psychological peer with your grandchild, the role of wizard makes you an almost mystical superior. You may find that it is one of the most enjoyable for you to play, and one of the most wondrous for your grandchildren. That's because, for your grandchildren, especially those under the age of seven, you can provide an imaginative and somewhat magical counterpoint to their otherwise busy, task-oriented, day-to-day worlds. Unlike parents and teachers, you are not bound to enforce the concepts of duty and discipline with your grandchildren—although you may exemplify these concepts. Consequently, you can indulge your grandchild's fantasies more than parents or other authority figures can.

Actually, fantasies are not luxuries but necessities for children, particularly around the ages of four and five. Dr. Jerome L. Singer, a professor of psychology at Yale University and the author of *The House of Make-Believe,* maintains that there is a deep human need for fantasy throughout life, but that young children especially benefit from imaginative play. He says that those who are not encouraged in this area, or who spend too much time passively watching television, end up being aggressive and getting into fights. Other studies have shown that children who are adept at make-believe prove to have enhanced intellectual skills, are more complex than average, and display above-average verbal skills. They are also more emotionally balanced. So let yourself be your grandchild's guide to the preternatural world of make-believe and illusion, of dreams and surprises.

How can you do that? Children's capacity to appreciate wonder is infinite! Even such seemingly mundane tasks as letting dough rise for a loaf of bread or making a garden grow can be magical for small children. One grandfather I spoke with described a game he plays with his grandson in which he operates the car headlights, windshield wipers, and horn with "magic from his fingertips." In reality, he points at the instruments with one finger while he secretly switches them on with his other hand. He hasn't told his amazed grandson his secret yet. And why should he? When your grandchildren come to see you as a magical person, it further solidifies you as distinct and unique for them, and cements their perception of you as different from their parents. With your tricks and your talents and the twinkle in your eye, you can transport your grandchildren to a wonderland.

10. HERO
As a wizard, you are a magical creature. There is one last role, however, and in this one you seem not so much otherwordly as larger than life. You can be your grandchild's hero. For one thing, your grandchildren instinctively sense that you possess profound powers of authority over their parents. As one youngster told me, "Who else can boss my parents around?"

While it may seem that the fulfillment of this role comes at the expense of the parents, the fact is that your grandchildren genuinely need you to negotiate with their parents. Sometimes your grandchildren will expect you to directly intervene for them. Knowing that you can "boss the parents around" gives your grandchildren a bit of clout and an emotional safety valve. This kind of safety valve is especially important for teenagers feuding with their parents. Many teenagers I know use Grandma and Grandpa's house for an emotional sanctuary. One troubled teen told me, "I'll never have to go on the street if I fight with my parents or to a mental hospital if I crack up. I can always go to my grandmother's house until things cool down." This kind of arrangement usually works well as long as grandparents are careful not to undermine parental authority too much, and as long as parents keep a sense of humor.

Beyond this practical aspect of your role as hero, though, there is a more enchanting one. Your grandchild almost certainly views your past life, so far removed from her own everyday experience, as having heroic qualities. That's why she loves to hear your stories. Grandparents who have come from foreign lands, who saw Babe Ruth play, who had exciting jobs and adventures, who travel, who know other languages, usually are far more exciting to children than the plastic superhero dolls they play with. Think of the heroic stature, in his granddaughter's eyes, of one grandfather I know who was attacked by and managed to kill a grizzly bear! Particularly in this era of fallen idols, when we no longer have heroic examples as heads of state, when sports superstars are victims of AIDS, and when the tabloids exploit every lurid detail of the lives of people in the public eye, your grandchildren need you as someone to look up to.

If that seems like a tall order at this point in your life, remember that even your infirmities can be intriguing and inspiring for your grandchildren. Swollen joints, wrinkles, and missing teeth and the stories that go with them are fascinating to children. They even like to visit the doctor with you. Keep in mind that every bump, wrinkle, and scar has a story. Even if there are no stories to go along with the scars, there's always the possibility of making some up. Many of the grandparents with whom I spoke told me that part of their heroism included stretching the truth a bit when they shared stories with their grandchildren. By embellishing reality, grandparents are able to open a child's mind and broaden the child's experiences. So can you. But enlivening a child's imagination doesn't mean lying to the child. You can always make a midstream correction in the tale when your grandchild reaches the age of reason. The important thing is to let them revere you as a hero during the early years when they need you in that role.

There you have it: ten wonderful ways for you to interact with your grandchildren. There are two other ways, however, and each is so important that it deserves an entire chapter unto itself. First comes how you and your grandchildren—in spite of the span of years between you—can become healthier and more physically fit as a result of being together.

3

Body Building

I n 1985, a full 71 percent of 9 million U.S. children
between the ages of six and seventeen failed to meet
the fitness standards for an "average healthy youngster" set forth by the Amateur Athletic Union, the country's largest nonprofit organization dedicated to
promoting physical fitness. Not only that, but researchers
at the Harvard School of Public Health showed that by
1980, the number of obese children in the United States
had risen 53 percent since 1963 and the number who fell
into the "super obese" category had risen 98 percent.
Also, a study done in the late 1980s by the President's
Council on Physical Fitness and Sports reported: "Upper
arm and shoulder muscle girdle strength and endurance

for both boys and girls was poor. It remains a significant weakness in our youth. Many have insufficient strength to handle their own body weight in case of emergency, and were judged as being often unable to carry on daily work or physically demanding recreational activities successfully or safely." Translation: Today's children are out of shape—dangerously so.

Why? Experts point to two factors: Youngsters these days ride instead of walk, and they often come home to a latchkey existence that encourages a passive and pernicious time passer—namely, watching television. According to a recent report from the National Children and Youth Fitness Study, 72.3 percent of grade school children watch up to two hours of TV on schooldays, and another 27 percent watch between three and five hours. That leaves only .7 percent of children who watch under two hours a day. As for the weekends, 28.3 percent of the children watch up to two hours of TV, 61 percent watch three to five hours, and more than 10 percent watch six or more hours a day. And of course, when they're not watching the tube, a preponderance of youngsters are absorbed in yet another sedentary pastime: video games. Leaving aside the deplorable content of much of what the kids see on TV and the search-and-destroy aspect of many video games, just the simple fact that our children are inactive for a majority of their young lives is appalling enough.

But what has all of this got to do with you? Plenty. I'm going to put you in charge of your grandchildren's health and fitness. As a first step, we're going to get you involved in a sensible—and fun—intergenerational exercise program. Yet I have a feeling that you're skeptical about your ability to act as your grandchild's unofficial workout buddy "at your age."

Let's Get Moving

Don't be. Grandparenting should not be a spectator sport. No matter how you feel now, no matter how out of shape you are, you *can* improve your physical condition if you work at it. Consider the results of a study reported in the *Journal of the American Medical Association* in 1990. A group of nursing home residents between the ages of ninety and ninety-six, all of them frail and many in wheelchairs, underwent eight weeks of intense physical therapy involving weights and resistance training. The results were astonishing. All of the subjects showed marked improvement in functional mobility and significant gains in muscular size and strength. Some who had not walked unaided for years rose up out of their wheelchairs and began to take daily strolls around the grounds of the residence. All of this in only eight weeks! Just imagine how much physical power and agility you could gain if you made a long-range commitment to a fitness program with your grandchildren.

There are other benefits of engaging in regular, moderate exercise, regardless of age. For one thing, exercise has been shown to increase cardiovascular fitness. If you, like most people, think this is only important for adults, you're wrong. According to the Department of Health, more than 40 percent of the children in this country between the ages of five and eight already show risk factors for heart disease, such as high blood pressure and high levels of cholesterol. Exercise is a key factor in reversing these problems, and therefore promoting longevity. Christopher Peterson, author of *Health and Optimism,* sees this as a motivating factor in getting people of any age to make the effort to exercise. He also points out that in his research, the vital people are often those who take the best care of themselves, simply because they love life and want to live as fully as humanly possible.

Doreen Gluckin, M.D., author of *The Body at Thirty,* would heartily agree. "We need to be active," says Dr. Gluckin. "If our muscles are trim and in good tone, our heart and lungs conditioned, our body weight normal and constant at that level, and if we have a regular exercise program, we will have far fewer health problems, and we may not age as rapidly. These measures will keep calcium in our bones, our bursae free and well lubricated, our tendons firm and strong, and our joint cartilage well-nourished."

All of her points are well taken, but let's focus for a moment on the mention of "calcium in our bones." Weight-bearing exercise—which includes just about everything except swimming—helps prevent loss of bone density, a condition that often leads to osteoporosis. This debilitating affliction most often affects postmenopausal women because of a diminished supply of circulating estrogen—the hormone which, among other things, promotes bone density. However, sedentary men can also fall prey to osteoporosis. The condition is progressive, and in later stages can result in bones so fragile that just standing up can cause broken hips or "crush fractures" of the vertebrae. Also, both men and women are more prone to the problem if they were inactive as children and young people, which is why you want to get your grandchildren up and moving right now. Jaqueline G. Parthmore, M.D., chief of staff at the Veterans Administration Hospital in San Diego, California, says that people continue to accumulate bone mass until about the age of thirty. "Since life expectancy is now close to eighty—as opposed to forty, which was the case a hundred years ago," she says, "we have to have enough to last us through our thirties and forties, and then well past that time."

Dr. Parthmore says that moderate and regular weight-bearing exercise is essential in promoting peak bone density, and points out that astronauts in a weightless environment experience significant loss of bone density. This last assertion is corroborated in the sixteenth edition of the *Merck Manual of Diagnosis and Therapy,* which recommends as a treatment for the pain accompanying crush fractures "hyperextension exercises to strengthen flabby paravertebral muscles." The manual goes on to say that in spite of the pain experienced by patients, "immobilization should be minimized and a consistent exercise regimen encouraged, since exercise is vital for healthy bone."

So exercise is not only good for your muscles, but weight-bearing exercise makes strong bones as well. Yet is it also possible that movers and shakers have a more efficient immune response than sedentary people do? James M. Rippe, M.D., director of the Exercise Physiology and Nutrition Laboratory of the University of Massachusetts Medical Center in Worcester, and editor-in-chief of a periodical called *Medicine, Exercise, Nutrition and Health,* thinks the answer is yes. "The link is there," says Dr. Rippe. "For one thing, the body temperature rises slightly during exercise, and the immune system may interpret this as a mild fever, and marshal the infection-fighting cells."

In fact, a study done at Loma Linda University in California showed that moderate exercise strengthens the immune system by triggering the release of antibodies which attack viruses and bacteria. What's more, the brain chemicals called endorphins—a group of "inner opiates" which are natural pain relievers and mood elevators—may also signal the immune system to work harder.

I hope that by this point you're convinced that exercise is necessary and possible at any age. I hope you'll stop attributing every little ache and pain to aging—a practice which can in fact become a self-fulfilling prophecy that ends up accelerating the process. Once you are over the outdated notion that you are "too old" to be your grandchildren's fitness pal, you will see that you are the perfect person for this role. For one thing, as we have already established, your grandchild views you as the most fun adult in his life. Take advantage of this by coaxing him away from the TV and out into the fresh air for all kinds of games and activities that foster fitness—tag, jump rope, hopscotch, swimming, diving, stickball, badminton, biking, playing Frisbee, raking leaves, cross-country skiing, building a snowman—whatever suits you. You might also consider some organized activities. I know one grandmother who at age fifty-two enrolled in a "Mommy and Me" movement class at the Y with her three-year-old granddaughter.

"My daughter-in-law works, so she wasn't free to do this with Melanie, and I decided to give it a try," she says. "I felt like a fool the first day, in there with all those young mothers, but once we got going, I completely forgot about that. The teacher was terrific, really peppy and encouraging, and we did all kinds of stuff to music. Melanie's absolute favorite was 'Kitty Cats,' where we all got down on our hands and knees and arched our backs up and down, and then got up and ran around 'catching butterflies.' The teacher would say, 'There's one way over there!' and we were supposed to run across the room and then jump as high as possible and paw the air. We did this over and over until the music stopped. At the end, the whole class would just collapse on the floor, huffing and puffing and giggling. I've never had so much fun in my life, and to this day, I can hear Melanie's little-girl laughter. There's no other sound like it.

"Melanie's sixteen already, but she actually remembers that class perfectly. We have our little private joke, when we're in the backyard at a family barbecue. She'll whisper, 'Yo, Grandma, there's one way over there,' and we'll take off running and jumping and pawing and they all think we're nuts. But I'm sixty-five now, and I can still run and jump! That little class with Melanie really inspired me, and after she went to nursery school the next year, I enrolled in an aerobics class and I've been at it ever since. Also, Melanie has been figure skating since the age of five, and she's on the girls' soccer team. I like to think I got her started right."

Quite possibly, you—like this grandmother—are at a point in your life when you can afford to spend more leisure time with your grandchildren than the parents can, especially if they're both working. Particularly if you are retired or semiretired, you can devote plenty of hours to your grandchildren, but even if you are still employed full-time, you are not involved in the daily demands of child rearing and your time with the grandchildren can be reserved for pleasurable pursuits, not the least of which can be your personal exercise program. As one grandfather, a successful dentist, said to me, "When I was growing up, I played baseball. The coaches all told me I was a natural. I suppose I could have had a career, but I wasn't really interested. For one thing, I didn't like striking people out. That's just the way I am. But I also thought that I'd be a has-been by the time I was thirty. Back then, we all thought we'd be washed up physically at thirty, or certainly forty. And fifty! I had the idea I'd be hobbling around with a cane by then. Now I'm sixty-three, and the big surprise is that I'm in great shape. I jog every morning, and last year I started taking karate classes with my two grandsons who are eight and ten. We do this every Wednesday afternoon. I still have my dental practice, and I have no intention of retiring any-time soon—another surprise to me—but I make sure not to book any patients for that one afternoon a week. I owe that time to the boys and to myself. We all benefit, in more ways than one."

However, even though you too can benefit immensely from a fitness regimen with your grandchildren, regard-less of your age, you *must* get a complete physical before beginning, particularly if you've been warming the rock-ing chair a bit more than you should have lately. Actu-ally, the children should have a checkup as well. Then, once you've all been given the go-ahead, start slowly, building up and then maintaining as regular a schedule as possible—at least twenty minutes three times a week, and preferably thirty minutes or more five days a week.

There are several excellent books to guide you in this endeavor. Among the best are the following, which should be available in your local library:

• *The Family Fitness Handbook* by Rob Glover and Jack Shepherd. This is a thorough presentation of intergenerational exercise by best-selling fitness authorities. While grandparents are given short shrift, just ignore that problem and substitute "grandparent" every time you read "parent." Particularly valuable are the sections on fitness testing and family exercise, with tips on how to learn to play like a child and the "Three F's": fun, fellowship, and fitness.

• *Mommy & Me Exercises: The Kidnastics Program* by Christie Costanzo with Leo Costanzo. There are photographs and explanations for exercises involving children from birth to about six or seven. The newborn exercises are clearly labeled as such, and there is a pediatrician's foreword with safety guidelines. There is also a chapter called "And Daddy Makes Three." All you need to do is substitute "Grandma and Grandpa" for "Mommy and Daddy," and you've got yourself an intergenerational exercise program.

• *Exercise as You Grow Older* by Nona Kaufman, Naomi Lederach and Beth Lederach. The authors are an eighty-seven-year-old grandmother and her midlife daughter and teenage granddaughter. The book abounds with wit, wisdom, and verve, and there are plentiful photographs of these three women—"ordinary people" by their own description—engaging in intergenerational exercise. Especially uplifting is "Grandma's Chapter—Nona-Robics," in which Nona peppers her exercise instructions with down-home philosophy such as "You cannot make a peach out of a potato, but you can be improved!" and concludes with her own personal credo: "To my dear senior friends, may you somehow live bet-

ter and feel better because of the exercises recorded here.
... We have grown, changed and survived. We want to
keep on growing—without growth, there is no life. ...
Personally, I am sustained by my faith in an eternal God
... my interest in life and hope for tomorrow. My prayer
is, 'Lord, keep me alive as long as I live.' "

- *Staying Fit Past 50* by Cody Bartlett. This is an up-
to-the-minute guide, packed with information plus photographs of the fiftysomething author both before and
after he began working out.

One last word about exercise: No matter how careful
you are to warm up, go at a sensible pace, and then cool
down, there is still the possibility of incurring accidental
strains or sprains at any age. If you do pull something,
follow this advice from the sports medicine community.
Remember the word RICE:

Rest

Stop exercising immediately, and take at least seventy-
two hours off, even if you feel better the next morning.

Ice

Put ice cubes in a plastic bag and place it on the affected area for fifteen minutes at a time, with two-hour
breaks. Commercial gel packs which you put in the
freezer are not as effective as real ice. Neither are the
"pop packs" which make instant "ice," but these are inexpensive and good to have on hand if you're exercising
away from home—hiking or cross-country skiing or
whatever. Ice works by keeping excess blood from pool-

ing around the injury, thus preventing internal hema-
toma or bruises. (The only time you ever want to use
heat therapy is on the stiff and sore muscles surrounding an old injury. All the heat does is provide temporary pain relief and comfort. *Never* apply heat to a
fresh injury.)

Compression

Immediately wrap the affected area in an elastic bandage, being sure to adjust the pressure so that you don't
cut off circulation. Leave the bandage in place for fifteen
minutes, with two-hour breaks. You can combine this
therapy with the ice packs. Both measures keep blood
away from the injured site, discouraging swelling and
bruising.

Elevation

Get the injured site up higher than the nearest lymph
glands—located in the groin and the armpits. In other
words, prop an injured ankle or knee up on a pillow
above hip height, or rest an injured wrist above shoulder
level. Stay in this position while the ice and bandage are
in place.

This is an amazingly effective regimen. Naturally,
however, if anyone sustains a serious injury such as a
torn ligament or broken bone, you'll get medical attention immediately. However, don't let the fear of injury
keep you from exercising. You'll be *more* prone to injury
if you *don't* use your body than if you do. People who
are fit are less likely to turn an ankle stepping off a curb,
or wrench a shoulder shoveling snow, than inactive people are, and far less likely to suffer from stress fractures

and broken bones. So exercise prudently and tend to minor injuries on the spot, and you and the grandchildren will all be in fine shape.

Let Them Eat Smart

Exercise, of course, is only part of the formula for good health and fitness at any age. Another important element is proper nutrition. Research over the last ten years has dramatically changed recommendations for a prudent diet in this country, and if you are willing to learn what's new, you can serve as your grandchildren's role model and teacher. Actually, you would have had to be a hermit during the last decade to miss the fact that high-fat and high-cholesterol foods such as dairy products and red meat are out, while high-fiber and vitamin-rich foods such as fruits, vegetables, and grains are in. Still, change takes time, and if you grew up on a meat-and-potatoes regimen, you may have been reluctant to alter your eating habits. However, with your grandchildren's welfare to consider, it really is time to pay attention to the new rules. Even football players these days are finding fruits and veggies on the training table instead of steak and eggs. According to a recent poll conducted by the Foundation for Better Health in conjunction with the National Cancer Institute, twenty-three out of twenty-eight National Football League team trainers reported that their players eat twice the amount of fruits and vegetables as the average American male. Dean Klienschmidt, head athletic trainer for the New Orleans Saints, told *New York Newsday* reporter Bea Lewis that a produce man comes to the locker room at seven-thirty every morning and "unloads crates of bananas, apples, oranges, peaches and pears." And Heidi Skolnik, nutrition consultant for the New York Giants, gives cooking classes for the players and promotes an "overall shift in diet [with] less meat and more carbohydrates."

What's the result of this kind of eating? First, studies have shown that the new nutrition promotes a reduced risk of cancer and cardiovascular disorders. And a generous intake of leafy green vegetables also serves as the best source (better than dairy products) of calcium to ward off osteoporosis. No one is exactly sure just how all of this works, but in a variety of ways, high-carb/low-fat eating marshals the body's natural defenses against disease.

The human immune system is a squadron of antibodies that battles to keep us from falling prey to the countless bacteria and viruses we come into contact with every day of our lives. The scientific community believes that a regimen of good nutrition—along with exercise and a reduction in stress—can turn the immune system into an even more powerful force against disease. By starting right now to teach your grandchildren how to eat right, you'll be giving them a lifetime lesson in how to protect themselves against nuisance ailments like allergies and the common cold as well as such potential killers as cancer and heart disease. I realize that the parents are the ones mainly in charge of the youngsters' diet, but statistics show that the middle generation has already become enthusiastic about the new nutrition, and you will probably find that you are simply bolstering what the grandchildren learn at home when you serve them a wholesome diet at your house, or encourage them to order good food when you eat out. Why not have a family council on this topic to see if all generations can concur on the best ways to eat smart? Getting the kids involved in these discussions is important, since they are much more likely to eat right when they are informed and have a say in the matter than when they are simply ordered to "eat your vegetables" and "clean your plate."

One charming story which illustrates this fact involves a four-year-old girl who was visiting her grandparents for a week one summer. The child had been brought up on a wholesome diet of fish, vegetables, fruit, and pasta, and she didn't much like her grandmother's cooking, which involved lots of rich, spicy sauces. Also, the grandmother heaped the child's plate and set it down in front of her, whereas back home the little girl was allowed to serve herself from platters on the table. On the third day of the visit, the grandmother got thoroughly exasperated as the child yet again picked and prodded at her food and barely touched it.

"No dessert tonight unless you eat everything on your plate!" the grandmother scolded.

"But Grandma," said the child, "how did you know how much to put on it in the first place?"

Out of the mouths of babes. Happily, this grandmother was a good sport, and willing to learn. She had a hearty laugh over the situation. The next day, she and the child cooked dinner together, tasting and testing as they went, and the child was allowed to fill her own plate. Sure enough, she ate with gusto that evening. And this grandmother was also open-minded enough to consult her daughter-in-law about the child's customary diet, and to readjust her own thinking about nutrition. As a result, the grandmother lost weight and feels better than she has in years.

This case underscores the fact that the right diet really

can make *all* of you stay healthier. Here is a short course
in which nutrients do the most to promote general good
health and boost the immune system, based on the information in *Immune for Life* by Arnold Fox, M.D., and
Barry Fox and in Consumer Guide's *Vitamins for a
Healthy Life.*

Vitamins

Vitamin A is the most important nutrient for enabling
the immune system to function efficiently. This vitamin
is essential for the growth and repair of cells, including
the lymphocytes which fight disease. Also, vitamin A for-
tifies the skin as well as the linings of the lungs, esoph-
agus, stomach, intestine, colon, rectum, gallbladder,
kidneys, and urinary tract, all of which act to block ma-
rauding bacteria and viruses. This is why a sign of vitamin A deficiency is an increased susceptibility to infections. Make sure you all get a good supply of this
immune-boosting nutrient by serving carrots and spinach, as well as other yellow or leafy green vegetables—
pumpkins or squash, sweet potatoes, yams, kale, water-
cress, collards, turnip greens—and fruits like apricots.

Second only to vitamin A when it comes to boosting
the immune system is vitamin B_6 (pyridoxine), which is
found in virtually all fruits and vegetables, particularly
bananas. Be careful not to destroy the vitamin by over-
cooking foods, because without this nutrient, another
essential immune-boosting vitamin, B_{12}, cannot be
absorbed. The double loss interferes with the formation
of red blood cells and impairs the functioning of the
nervous system, both of which can make you and your

family vulnerable to illness. If anyone complains of numbness or tingling in arms and legs and/or has frequent cracks and sores around the mouth, a B_6/B_{12} deficiency is probably the cause.

The rest of the B family of vitamins comes next on the list of special immune-boosting nutrients, and they also help prevent depression, an emotional disorder which, of course, can in turn promote physical illness. Vitamin B_1 (thiamine) is found in legumes (beans, peas, nuts), grains (cereals, breads, pasta), and milk and milk products (yogurt, cottage cheese, cheese). Vitamin B_2 (riboflavin) is found in liver, spinach, milk, and milk products; vitamin B_3 (niacin) is found in turkey, chicken, fish, milk, and milk products; and vitamin B_5 (pantothenic acid) is found in all foods. Vitamin B_{12} is found in fish—and meat, cheese, and eggs as well, but these are not your best choices because of the high cholesterol content.

What about vitamin C? In spite of the controversial megadose theories put forth by Dr. Linus Pauling in the late 1970s, vitamin C really *is* important in boosting the immune system, because it strengthens the action of key lymphocytes. With a proper intake of vitamin C, wounds heal faster and symptoms of the common cold are less troublesome. Remember, though, that colds cannot actually be *prevented* by an intake of vitamin C.

Remember, too, that vitamin C is not manufactured by the human body, which is why sailors (later dubbed "Limeys") developed scurvy until they began adding limes and other citrus fruits to the food cargo on their long sea voyages. So make sure your family gets a daily serving or two from the following list: oranges, lemons, limes, grapefruit, melons, berries, tomatoes, and spinach.

Last on the list of immune boosters is vitamin E (to-copherol). Found in vegetable and seed oils for cooking and dressings and in whole-grain cereals, this vitamin improves the functioning of the immune system in two ways. First, it protects body cells from destruction by oxidation, and second, it helps control "free radicals," the unstable molecules that cause cancer, among other disorders. Vitamin E also keeps individual cell membranes strong, and encourages healing.

Keep in mind, however, that the human body needs a balanced diet in order to stay healthy. Each vitamin and other micronutrients such as zinc and copper work best when the other essential nutrients are present as well.

But what about supplements? They are superfluous if people truly eat a balanced diet. Unfortunately, most people, especially children, won't succeed in doing that every day. This is a good argument for supplements, but don't fall for the megadose theories, particularly when you're dealing with oil-based vitamins such as A and D. These are stored in the body rather than eliminated and can actually be poisonous in large quantities.

Still, as we've said, the surest way to get a supply of immune-boosting vitamins and minerals is to eat foods that contain them. As a rule of thumb, these immune-boosting foods are better in their natural form. In other words, an apple is better than apple juice because the whole fruit provides fiber and micronutrients which are lost in processing. Similarly, whole-grain products have fiber and B vitamins, and even the "enriched" white breads and rice products don't restore all of the natural benefits of the original—particularly fiber, which promotes good digestion and may prevent colon cancer.

Fat

The first rule is to teach children that sweets are empty calories which do nothing but promote overweight. There's nothing wrong with letting a child enjoy an occasional piece of Grandma's apple pie, or a slice of birthday cake with ice cream, or some Halloween candy. But these should be presented as very special treats and not as everyday staples. Keep in mind that a study by Rujik Chandra, M.D., of the University of Newfoundland has shown that childhood obesity is a significant factor in compromising the immune system.

On the other hand, an important way to boost a child's immune system is to limit fat intake from a very early age, sometime between the second and fourth birthday. One recent study in particular, done by the American Health Foundation in New York City, showed that a low-fat diet allows certain immune-system cells, the so-called Natural Killers or NK's, to act at peak efficiency. James R. Hebert, M.D., an author of the study and now an epidemiologist at the University of Massachusetts, explains that a high-fat diet causes the NK's to get "fat and lazy." For the short term, this has the effect of making kids susceptible to such problems as colds, flu, and earaches, while in the long run, people with inefficient NK's may be at risk for heart disease and cancer.

"We consistently saw a significant suppression of NK activity in subjects on a diet of over 20 percent fat," says Dr. Hebert. "We were studying young adults, but I see no reason that the findings cannot be applied to children. The important thing to remember is that an excess in the diet of *any* type of fat—even polyunsaturated vegetable oils—will contribute to inhibiting the NK response."

However, the experts all caution against limiting fat intake before a child is two years old. During the period from birth to age two, when rapid brain growth occurs, youngsters do need more than 30 percent of their calories from fat. The best source of this for infants is breast milk. And while formula is an acceptable substitute in the fat department, researchers have long known that a breast-fed baby also gets antibodies from the mother to help the baby's own immature immune system. Now, new research done independently by Michael H. Julius at McGill University in Montreal and Armond G. Good at the University of Texas Medical Branch in Galveston points to the possibility that a certain maternal protein in breast milk may "teach" the infant's system how to develop an immune response of his own. So support your daughter or daughter-in-law in her desire to breast-feed your newborn grandchildren.

But whether the source of infant nutrition is breast milk or formula, whole milk should be the first step after weaning, with low-fat milk not introduced until the third year.

Protein

Another immune-boosting nutrient for youngsters is protein. Overall, the best advice seems to be to offer kids low-fat protein sources such as chicken, fish, veal, and lean cuts of beef, as well as low-fat dairy products, plus soy products and peanut butter. Stay away from pork and marbled beef. Also, charcoal-broiled foods and those that are smoked or prepared with nitrates and nitrites, such as hot dogs, may promote cancer, so limit them.

However, there's no need to become fanatical about banning hamburgers and hot dogs altogether, especially if the kids really won't eat the other options. Adequate protein is absolutely essential, and William G. Bithoney, M.D., associate chief of general pediatrics and director of the Growth and Nutrition Clinic at Children's Hospital in Boston and professor of pediatrics at Harvard Medical School, warns against a diet that satisfies a child's appetite pretty much exclusively with carbohydrates. The result can be a condition called Protein-Calorie Undernutrition (PCU), which invites pneumonia, bacteremia, and wound and urinary tract infections.

Stress Busting

Not surprisingly, however, nutrition is only part of the puzzle when it comes to keeping immune systems in good shape. As we have already seen, exercise is a contributing factor. Still, the measurable physical effects of exercise are not the whole story. For one thing, exercise also acts as a self-esteem builder, which promotes overall good health. "Kids who are building their bodies are also building self-esteem," says exercise expert Dr. Rippe. "The connection between the mind and the body is undeniable."

Dr. Rippe goes on to say that exercise also acts as a stress reliever and that the connection between stress and the immune response has been well documented. A long-term, ongoing study by Janice K. Kiecolt-Glaser at Ohio

State University in Columbus showed that subjects in a stressful role, such as caregivers for Alzheimer's patients, had measurably weaker immune systems than did control subjects, and significantly more depression and infectious illnesses. Further trials showed that people in stressful situations who had the love and support of family members had stronger immune responses than those who were criticized by the important people in their lives. The latter group—those in stressful situations who got only negative feedback for their efforts—had the poorest immune response of all subjects. I don't have to tell you that as a grandparent, you are the perfect adult to offer your grandchildren the positive feedback and unconditional love which can serve to bolster their defense against illness.

Other research has shown independently that undue stress can cause the immune system to be either underactive or overactive. The first response can lead to upper respiratory infections and other ills, while the latter causes allergies. Bearing this out, one recent study, done by psychologist Glenda McQueen at McMaster University in Canada, showed that laboratory animals could be "trained" to have an allergic reaction to stress. The rats were injected with a known allergen such as egg white and simultaneously subjected to loud noises and flashing lights. Later trials showed that the rats developed physical allergic symptoms when exposed *only* to the lights and sounds. So stress can literally make us sick. But you knew that. That's why your natural urge to grandparent prompts you to comfort your grandchildren in times of stress, to take their side, cuddle them, praise them, make them laugh and feel special. No one can do this better than you can.

Grandma and Grandpa Know Best

However, as a grandparent who has already raised a family of your own, you also already know that there's more to keeping a child healthy than just exercise, good nutrition, and stress reduction. Some old-fashioned common sense is important, too. Louis Z. Cooper, M.D., director of pediatrics at St. Lukes–Roosevelt Hospital in New York City and professor of pediatrics at the College of Physicians and Surgeons at Columbia University, urges adults to trust their instincts when it comes to children's health. "For example, there's no empirical evidence about the relationship between sleep and the immune system, but everyone knows that kids who don't get enough sleep are 'rundown,' " says Dr. Cooper. "People also know that each child needs a different amount of sleep, and has different daily rhythms."

As a general guideline, however, children need more sleep than adults do. At age six, most youngsters require almost eleven hours a night, say experts, with sleep time gradually declining to nine hours for twelve-year-olds.

Dr. Cooper goes on to remind us that teaching time-honored rituals for good hygiene—having kids wash hands before and after they eat and after using the bathroom, and instructing them to avoid putting their fingers in their mouths and eyes—still goes a long way toward warding off common illnesses. Naturally, if your youngest grandchildren are in day care, you'll want to encourage the parents to be sure that the caregivers are fastidious about good hygiene habits.

Also, use your grandparent power to encourage the

children to take good care of their teeth. One grand-mother remembers the Christmas when her grandson was five and her granddaughter was three. Almost as an afterthought while shopping for the children's presents, she bought an inexpensive pair of toothbrush and cup holders, one in the shape of a duck and the other in the shape of an elephant. These gifts proved to be the hit of Christmas morning, and the grandmother says that after all the presents had been opened, the scene was this: Grandpa and Daddy were struggling to put together an elaborate train set, Mommy and Aunt Sue were fussing over a baby doll with an extensive wardrobe and a bi-zarre repertoire of skills having to do with the alimentary canal—and the children were upstairs in the bathroom, gleefully brushing their teeth over and over, quacking and trumpeting and giggling as they went.

"This really tickled me," says the grandmother. "But I was seriously pleased that they were into brushing. So the next year, I gave them each a travel case with a little fold-up toothbrush and a tiny tube of toothpaste, just like the one I carry in my purse. I encouraged them to brush after lunch at school. And when they were a little older, we had flossing sessions together. See, kids think anything's a game and anything's fun, especially if Grandma is in on it!"

Thank You for Not Smoking

Of course, that fact can work against you as well. If you set a bad example by smoking, the kids may well want to follow your lead just as they would follow a good example. Something else to keep in mind, however: Stud-ies have shown that secondary smoke, or the "passive smoking" which occurs when nonsmokers inhale what smokers around them exhale, has serious adverse effects on the immune response, particularly of children in households where people smoke. These kids are statistically much more prone to upper respiratory illnesses such as colds and bronchitis, and this can make them "rundown" and thus susceptible to anything else that's going around. If you and/or the parents or other grandparents still smoke, why not let the birth of this precious new generation spur you to make every effort to quit—for the children's sake as well as your own. Perhaps all of the adult smokers in the family could join a support group together. After all, passive smoking is not the only problem. For one thing, if your daughter or daughter-in-law smokes, there is a danger to the unborn child. And again if you smoke, you are frankly abusing your role as the hero of your grandchild's eye. You are setting a precedent and giving him the idea that smoking is "grown-up" and desirable.

Thinking About Drinking

While we're on the subject of heroes and role models, we need to discuss alcohol. America has historically had a love/hate relationship with drinking. As social historian Mark Lender points out, every culture has a drug of choice—the coca leaf in South America, opium in China, alcohol in America. Yet even though our first colonists were seasoned drinkers who loved to point out that alcohol was safer than the water, by the early 1900s our newly industrialized society began to frown on drinking. By 1916, largely due to the efforts of Carrie Nation, the six-foot-tall grandmother who spearheaded the temperance movement, twenty-three states were "dry." By 1920, the whole country had Prohibition. Yet the "Noble Experiment" lasted a mere thirteen years during which bootleggers, speakeasies, and bathtub gin slaked the thirst of millions who blithely ignored the law. Still, when Prohibition was finally repealed, Americans did statistically drink less for several decades than they had prior to that. Even so, drinking has steadily increased, and today we drink an annual total of 5.75 billion gallons of beer (about 55 six-packs per person) and another billion gallons of wines and spirits, for a total cost of close to $80 billion.

Given these numbers, it's no wonder many kids point to their parents and teachers and coaches as hypocrites. "Adults do it. Why can't we?" said one fourteen-year-old girl when she gave an anonymous interview to *Long Island Newsday* reporter Rahel Musleah for a Sunday, March 29, 1992, article entitled "High School Students Flock to Keg Parties." This is a refrain heard in homes and schools everywhere, and variations on it are quoted in articles around the country on the teen drinking problem. And the problem is severe. Consider these statistics:

- One out of every three teens has had trouble at home, in school, or with the law because of alcohol.

- Nine out of ten high school seniors drink.

- The average age when boys begin drinking is eleven; for girls, it's 12.7.

- Kids drink to get drunk, averaging five or more beers in a row, usually on an empty stomach.

• The incidence of underage binge drinking is the highest it's been in twelve years.

The reason these facts are so alarming is that while most adults do drink, an estimated 90 percent drink responsibly. Kids simply don't. Brad Casemore, administrator of Brighton Hospital's twenty-bed Adolescent Treatment Center in Michigan, said, "They don't tend to drink as often as adults, but when they drink, they drink a heck of a lot. . . . Very few young people drink to have just one or two drinks."

Not only that, but kids are not finished growing, either physically or emotionally. That being so, a child's response to alcohol is empirically different from an adult's. In an article by Amelia M. Arria and others in *Alcohol Health and Research World* in 1991, the authors stress that while the current teen alcohol problem calls for much more research than has been done on the subject, all of the studies done so far have shown problems with bone growth, neurological impairment, emotional instability, early liver damage, impaired absorption of nutrients, suppression of the immune response, and endocrine imbalance in youngsters who use alcohol. In addition, a study done by psychiatrist Laure Ruydens Branchey of the Veterans Administration Medical Center in New York City showed that alcoholics whose drinking problems emerge before the age of twenty are much more likely to experience clinical depression, attempt suicide, and spend time in jail for crimes.

So whether or not adults should drink or do drink seems to be a moot point. What matters is that *kids* shouldn't. That being so, if you do drink, you will certainly want to educate your grandchildren about age-appropriate alcohol use, and discuss alcohol abuse as well.

For help in doing so, you can write for free literature from the following organizations. Those with asterisks will also provide educational materials about preventing drug abuse in youngsters, a problem which currently cuts across ethnic and socioeconomic lines and is particularly prevalent in well-to-do suburbs where latchkey kids and teens have plenty of spending money and far too little supervision.

The Center for Science in the Public Interest publishes a *Healthletter* and offers a videotape from the Coalition on Alcohol Advertising and Family Education entitled "Health Messages in Alcohol Ads."

1875 Connecticut Ave. NW, Suite 300
Washington, DC 20009-5728
(202) 332-9110

The Century Council is a nonprofit organization dedicated to reducing alcohol abuse and misuse across the United States, offers an excellent package of educational pamphlets as well as posters for merchants. The campaign is called "Here's Looking at You, Kid."

1999 Ave. of the Stars, Suite 2050
Los Angeles, CA 90067
(310) 557-9898

The U.S. Department of Health and Human Services has a series of eight survey reports collectively entitled

"Youth and Alcohol: A National Survey": (1) "Drinking Habits, Access, Attitudes and Knowledge"; (2) "Do They Know What They're Drinking?"; (3) "Drinking and Crime"; (4) "Dangerous and Deadly Consequences"; (5) "A Sample of Enforcement and Prevention Programs"; (6) "Controlling Alcohol Advertising That Appeals to Youth"; (7) "Laws and Enforcement: Compendium of State Laws"; and (8) "Laws and Enforcement: Is the 21-Year-Old Drinking Age a Myth?" There are also many other related materials, under the auspices of the National Institute on Drug Abuse, available from the same address.

5600 Fishers Lane
Rockville, MD 20857
(301) 443-6245

MADD (Mothers Against Drunk Driving) publishes a newsletter and offers a pamphlet called "Parent's Guide to Sober Teen Celebrations" as well as information on how to start a local chapter.

National Office
P.O. Box 541688
Dallas, TX 75354-1699
(214) 744-MADD

The National Clearinghouse for Alcohol and Drug Information has a computerized network of all types of services, speakers, and educational materials available around the country.

P.O. Box 2345
Rockville, MD 20852
(800) 729-6686, ext. 260

SADD (Students Against Drunk Driving) publishes a
newsletter and offers a pamphlet entitled "Celebrate Life:
Prom and Graduation Activities," as well as information
on how to start a local chapter.

P.O. Box 800
Marlboro, MA 01752
(508) 481-3568

*Target, the Substance Abuse Prevention Services
component of the National Federation of State High
School Associations* offers materials and on-site workshops for extracurricular groups such as cheerleaders,
kick lines, and football and soccer teams.

11724 NW Plaza Circle
P.O. Box 20626
Kansas City, MO 64195-0626
(800) 366-6667, (816) 464-5400

Also, in thinking about your own drinking, bear in
mind that the latest research on adult intake and risk,
particularly for women, is conflicting. More than a dozen
recent studies have linked moderate drinking in postmenopausal women with an increase in the risk for
breast cancer. However, other studies have shown that
moderate drinking, particularly of red wine, can reduce
the risk of heart disease for both men and women of all

ages. By the way, "moderate" in all of these studies was defined as two drinks a day for men and one drink a day for women. A drink was defined as one 12-ounce beer, or one 4- or 5-ounce glass of wine, or one 1-ounce shot of hard liquor.

Needless to say, if you have grown accustomed over the years to consuming considerably more than that, you would do well to face this fact and make the choice to change your drinking habits—for your sake as well as for your grandchildren's.

Sex and Your Grandchildren

Being honest about alcohol and drugs with your grandchildren isn't easy, but talking about sexuality is even more difficult. However, in the age of AIDS, you really have no choice but to broach the subject. As a responsible and caring grandparent, you should read the latest findings about AIDS as well as other sexually transmitted diseases and birth control, and be prepared to discuss these topics with your grandchildren. As Dr. Ruth Westheimer once said, grandparents have a far easier time talking with youngsters about sex than parents do, particularly if the parents are divorced and therefore dating themselves.

True, most schools now have sex education, but nothing can replace the wisdom and love you can impart when talking with your grandchildren about this all-important aspect of their young lives. It's a good idea to visit the school and find out what your grandchildren are being taught so that you can supplement the material and correct any misunderstandings. The main point is that you can't leave the whole job to the schools, largely because the programs don't seem to be doing much good. Surgeon General Joycelyn Elders reports that of the 56 million Americans with sexually transmitted diseases, nearly 17 percent are teenagers. Teenagers also have 350,000 abortions every year, and the teenage birthrate, which had dropped in the 1970s and early '80s, has been rising steadily since 1986. Also, government surveys show that more than half of American adolescents, both boys and girls, become sexually active before they turn seventeen. So don't assume that your grandchildren will be wise enough to abstain. Talk to them. One boy, who adores his grandmother, was quite taken aback when she brought up the subject of sex, but he listened intently.

"She really set me straight on that one when I was seventeen," he laughed. "She came right out and asked me if I was doing it with my girlfriend, who was fifteen at the time. I kind of fumbled, and then I said yes. But Grandma didn't get mad or anything. First she asked me if we used condoms, and I was honest and said sometimes yes, but sometimes we got carried away. Then Grandma told me a bunch of stuff about how condoms are important, but that even then you're not as safe as you think. She had read up on AIDS and she told me the virus could get through a condom. I knew that, but just hearing her say it made an impression on me. She also said if you get a girl pregnant you could be ruining your chances to go to college and make something of yourself. She had plenty of stories about people she had known in her day who had to get married or had back-alley abortions. She really made an impression on me. You know, the voice of experience.

"And she really does care about my future. She has saved some money for my college education even though she's living on a fixed income and is in her eighties. So anyway, I just got this feeling that I couldn't let her down. Well, I broke up with my girlfriend the next year when I left for college, and I took my time getting involved with someone on campus. I didn't just sleep around like a lot of guys. Eventually in my sophomore year I met a terrific girl and we do sleep together but we're very careful. She's on the Pill and we also use a condom. I'm not taking any chances, not after what my grandmother told me."

Like this grandmother, you can find your own special and sincere way to encourage your grandchildren to abstain or at least to practice safe sex. Don't shirk this job just because it makes you uncomfortable. Here again, you are the adult who is in the best position to gain the child's respect and trust.

So, summing things up, adults and kids alike stay healthier if they eat right, exercise, get a reasonable amount of sleep, feel good about themselves, practice safe sex and proper hygiene, including oral hygiene, don't smoke, and don't abuse alcohol and other drugs. As a grandparent, you can play a significant role in assuring that your grandchildren follow these vital precepts. What better motivation for making the grandparent years a period of increased wellness and vigor for yourself as well? After all, if you do, you'll stand a far better chance of living long enough to fulfill what is really your most important grandparental role of all, that of spiritual guide. This is a function of later life that has led Betty Friedan, now a seventy-two-year-old grandmother of eight and the author most recently of *The Fountain of Age,* to exhort people to stop denying old age by telling themselves they are still young. "It's a different stage of life, and if you are going to pretend it's youth, you are going to miss it," she told a *New York Times* reporter. "You are going to miss the surprises, the possibilities, the evolution."

These, then, are the years when your spirit comes into full flower. Share the miracle with your grandchildren—those brand-new beings who are only just beginning their own unique and remarkable adventures in the journey that is life.

4

That's the Spirit!

In the fall of 1993, Mel Lazarus's popular syndicated comic strip about Momma, a widowed grand-mother, showed Momma's son Thomas and her daughter-in-law Tina preparing to sell used household items. The dialogue was as follows:

Momma: "What's going on?"

Thomas: "A garage sale, Momma! We're getting rid of everything old and worthless that we no longer want."

Tina (depicted with a wicked grin as she points to an old chair displayed in the middle of the sale items): "Sit here, Mother Hobbs."

This is a chilling example of the lingering attitude in this country that older people, even if they are grandparents, have no role to play in the family or society. They are seen as worn-out, useless, and superfluous. Margaret Tallmer, a professor at Hunter College's Brookdale Center for the Aging, told a *New York Newsday* reporter, "Things are not geared to the life of the elderly and the message we send is that 'It would be easier if you left. You are an expense and you are not contributing to the Gross National Product.' "

At the same time, though—as the voracious baby boomer market approaches fifty—there is a Madison Avenue trend toward depicting the "new old" as age-defying pseudo–young people. Robust and beaming gray-haired models are pictured sporting tennis whites, or biking and backpacking. This may seem at first like a positive development, but on closer examination, I believe it only reinforces the idea that old age is not valuable *in and of itself.* Tracy Kidder, author of the best-selling book *Old Friends,* a study of growing old in America, concurs. He rails against replacing negative stereotypes of age with phony new stereotypes of "successful aging." Kidder—who did a great deal of on-site research in a nursing home—points out that the practice of portraying as role models only those older people who seem to have put aging on hold is not only daunting, but that it "leaves out a lot of people. . . . Eventually, of course, it leaves out everyone."

True, an entire chapter of this book has exhorted you to keep yourself in good physical shape as you grow older, but it was not meant to imply that doing so is the equivalent of finding the foutain of youth. It *is* important to be as healthy as possible in order to maintain the physical and mental tone to live your grandparent years to the fullest. If you feel good, think clearly, and are as free of pain and infirmities as possible, you will be able to enjoy your expanding spiritual knowledge, and impart it to your grandchildren. But there's no need to apologize for your age, or to deny it. Nor should you docilely accept society's painfully cute labels for older people, such as Golden Agers or Senior Citizens or Chronologically Gifted. On the contrary, you should be proud of having successfully arrived at this impressive benchmark in your life, and should think of yourself with respect. If we have to use a label at all, let it be Venerable Elder. You are, after all, a person of great knowledge and experience. However, while you have lived long enough to master many things, never forget that learning and growing should go on for as long as you live. Only that way will you remain eager to embrace the unforeseen experiences on the road not yet traveled.

Achieving this positive state of mind in a culture that devalues the elderly while simultaneously touting the benefits of anti-wrinkle creams, cosmetic surgery, and hair dyes, is a tremendous challenge, however. Then, too, along with the barrage of media messages, we have to cope with the physical *reality* of aging. One does eventually need reading glasses. Some people will need hearing aids. Arthritis can rob a person of the ability to perform simple tasks. A broken hip can mean a sudden loss of independence. There is also the fact that as we begin to look older, people treat us differently—sometimes with respect, but all too often in this society with pity and even abuse. One researcher, Patricia Moore, disguised herself as an elderly woman and traveled to 116 cities and towns from Florida to Canada over a three-year period in order to find out firsthand how older people are treated. She found that the vast majority of the time, she was considered a nuisance and was spoken to in patronizing terms. Once, while making a phone call in a Buffalo airport, she was knocked over by a man on his way to a boarding gate. Streams of people went by before someone finally helped her up. Ms. Moore had three disguises, one to make her look poor, one middle-class, and one affluent. Interestingly, the appearance of wealth made no difference in how she was treated. This fact squares with what my wife, Carol, has observed in her own unofficial survey of how people react to older women. Carol maintains that not only do people ignore elderly women, but that they show a real aversion to them, even turning to look the other way in order to avoid having to nod and smile while passing on the street.

Another researcher, David A. Karp, a professor of sociology at Boston College, has found that with each birthday there is an "increased pace of aging messages." "From about the age of fifty on, people are made to feel their age," Karp points out. His research, based on a theory called "symbolic interactionism," shows that the meanings attached to age are derived from interaction: that is, other people and situations provide a "looking-glass reflection" which defines who we are and sends specific messages forming our personal sense of how old we are. Karp holds that the inevitable "aging reminders" which crop up are fourfold: (1) family status shifts, such as becoming the parents of the bride or groom and then becoming grandparents; (2) other people's perceptions, such as when a young person calls you "ma'am" or your younger colleagues treat you with respect but don't include you when the gang goes out for a beer after work; (3) physical changes, such as wrinkles, gray hair, hair loss, and menopause; and finally, (4) intimations of mortality, as your AARP solicitation arrives in the morning mail, making you suddenly eligible for "senior" discounts. Then, too, the obituaries more and more often include people you knew and others your age or close to it, bringing you face to face with the reality that life on this earth does end.

These facts of later life do not have to be negative, however. In countries like Japan, where there has long been an annual observance called "Revere Your Elders Day," people accept aging with equanimity and even pride. But in this country, where the fairly recently instituted "Grandparents' Day" has yet to catch on as a real holiday and is little more than a sales opportunity for concerns such as greeting card companies, older people find it difficult to celebrate their status. And the situation is even worse for elders who are far from their families, particularly the widowed. Loneliness and a pervasive sense of not being needed anymore can invite dangerous depression. According to James J. Lynch, Ph.D., director of the Life Care Health Institute in Towson, Maryland, and the author of *The Broken Heart: Medical Consequences of Loneliness* and *The Language of the Heart: The Human Body in Dialogue,* the phrase "broken heart" is not just a metaphor. He reports that the rate of death from heart disease for people under the age of seventy who live alone is ten times greater than for others.

In addition, several recent studies have shown that close relationships have a direct, if still mysterious, effect on the immune system. For example, Sheldon Cohen, a psychologist at Carnegie Mellon University in Pittsburgh, and Jay Kaplan, a psychiatrist at Bowman Gray School of Medicine in Winston-Salem, North Carolina, writing in the September 1992 issue of the journal *Psychological Science,* conclude that "affiliation protects animals from the potentially pathogenic influence of chronic stress." Cohen and Kaplan did a long-range study of macaque monkeys in which some of the subjects were moved from cage to cage frequently, so that they never had a chance to bond with other monkeys. A control group was kept together in one cage throughout the trial. The latter showed great tenderness for one another and familial behavior such as cuddling up close and grooming each other, while the monkeys who had been moved from group to group had no affection for others. At the end of the trial the monkeys with no close relationships turned out to have seriously weakened immune systems, while the others had highly effective immune systems.

Cohen and Kaplan believe that the same would be true for humans, who are, after all, social animals. This is why loneliness and a sense of not being a valued part of the clan can cause severe depression, which in turn weakens the immune response and promotes illness. However, a growing number of the depressed elderly don't wait for disease to end their lives. A 1993 study by the Gallup Organization sponsored by Blue Cross/Blue Shield showed that suicide among Americans over sixty-five has been on the rise since the 1980s and that while this age group accounts for 26 percent of the population, the elderly commit an estimated 39 percent of the nation's suicides. According to Dr. Gene Cohen, acting director of the National Institute on Aging in Bethesda, Maryland, "The study highlights something that has been long known but overlooked: that the greatest rate of suicide is among the elderly."

Why? Hunter's Margaret Tallmer offers a sad but true comment about our priorities: "We value the young more than the elderly." Along with Dr. Gene Cohen, she theorizes that contributing factors in this alarming trend include financial problems, longer life spans, fears of being put away in a home, and isolation from friends and family. Listen to the poignant voice of one seventy-year-old woman who descended into a deep depression:

"Fifteen years ago, I was on top of the world. The youngest of our four children had just gone off to college, and my husband and I had sold our house in Connecticut and moved back to New York City, which is where we had lived as newlyweds. Selling the house was not an emotional issue for us. We had moved to the suburbs for the backyard and the good schools. And while we loved every minute of bringing up our kids, we had always looked forward to getting back to the city. George was a violinist who eventually got his degree and taught high school music, and I'm a pianist, so we both enjoyed being close to all the cultural goings-on. We got an apartment right near Carnegie Hall and Lincoln Center, and bought ourselves subscriptions to concerts, the opera, the ballet—the works.

"Anyway, George was ten years older than I, and he had retired in June of the year we moved. Two years later, he had a heart attack and died in the ambulance. I was with him, holding his hand. The grief was unspeakable. I had always known he would probably go first, yet I hadn't thought it would be so soon. But, well, you get on with life. I had plenty of friends—and then there was my teaching. I had given piano lessons ever since my first child was born, and as soon as we moved to the city, I had begun building a new clientele. So gradually I adjusted to life without George and I was basically content.

"I did worry about money, though. George had been collecting his TIAA CREF retirement checks, but we had selected the income option where he got quite a lot of money while he was alive but then the checks stopped when he died. We could have chosen the surviving-spouse option and collected less while he was alive, but that seemed silly at the time. We never thought he'd die so young. The upshot, of course, was that all I had after he was gone was my Social Security and the income from the piano lessons. There was also a small nest egg from the sale of the house, and we had saved a little even though we had never made a lot of money. The trouble was, my children all had student loans they were going to have to pay back, so for a long time they would be in no position to help me. In this economy, I figured they'd be lucky to make it on their own, without me as an extra burden. One day, I was walking along Seventh Avenue and I saw an old lady in a wheelchair. She was being pushed by a young woman in a white uniform. How could that old lady afford a paid companion? I got chills up and down my spine. What would happen to *me* if I couldn't get around on my own? After all, private companions are one thing, but even nursing homes cost a fortune these days. Anyway, the thought of going to a home just terrified me. I remembered visiting my Great-Aunt Ida at the Whispering Pines Home when I was a little girl in Missouri. Everything smelled faintly of urine and there were people moaning and the food looked just awful.

"I told a friend of mine about my fears, and she was only half joking when she said I should find myself a rich husband. But I never did start dating again. I kind of liked my freedom, and the solitude. After all those years with a house full of children and a man to pick up after and take care of as well, it was pleasant to have my little place all tidy, and just eat salads and listen to good music. And I was busy teaching. I loved the work, and I adored my little students! They were like grandchildren almost.

"Then, five years ago, I began to develop arthritis. I had aches and pains everywhere, but the worst of it was that my hands were affected. My hands! For a while, I could still play the piano, and the doctor said the exercise was good for my fingers, but then it got so I really couldn't play anymore. Oh, I could have gone on teaching, I suppose. Some people do it with a lot of talking and very little demonstrating. But that had never been my method. I couldn't stand not being myself, not being able to play so much as a scale with any real facility. So I stopped teaching. After that, I felt like my whole purpose in life was gone. I had brought up my children, and I couldn't play the piano or teach anymore. What earthly good was I?

"Oh yes, I had six grandchildren by then, but they all lived far away and they were so busy. We only got together about once a year, if that. Also, two of my children were divorced, and there were stepfathers and new in-laws and joint custody and all that confusion. You couldn't just say, 'Come home for Christmas.'

"I tried to cheer myself up by looking at the family album and listening to tapes of myself playing the piano in my prime, but those things only made me cry. I also tried telling myself that there were people a lot worse off than I was, people who were really sick or in debt or homeless. But that didn't seem to help. I felt sorry for everyone, but that didn't make me any happier. What was there to get up in the morning for? I figured maybe I had just outlived my usefulness. I hate to admit it, but at one point I thought about taking some pills and just getting it over with. I figured no one would miss me, anyway."

This woman's heartrending story illustrates a tragedy of national proportions. Like her, scores of older people have been robbed of either their physical prowess or their sense of being needed or both. As a result, they lose all hope. And hope is, in the words of Charles R. Snyder, a psychologist at the University of Kansas in Lawrence, "the prime mover of the human race." Without it, people give up. They go into a long-term depression which Dr. Snyder calls "psychological suicide," or they succumb to despair so totally that they actually commit suicide.

"Suicide is in effect the last goal," Dr. Snyder points out. "We have done a study of suicide notes which shows that people come to a decision, and then make careful plans, take concrete steps, and have high hopes of succeeding at this final act. The irony is that if you can catch a person just before she makes that firm decision, you can usually get her to see that she can put all that planning and energy into regaining hope and finding a new life goal instead of orchestrating her own death.

"But when I say 'hope,' I'm not talking about a child-like belief that everything is going to turn out all right," stresses Snyder, who conducted an in-depth study of seven thousand men and women between the ages of eighteen and seventy. He says that genuinely hopeful people quickly recognize an impossible dream for what it is, and they look for new, attainable goals suitable to the phase of life they are experiencing.

"They see life as a kind of game board," he maintains. "They are good strategists. They accept the fact that there will be obstacles, even dead ends. So they back up, look at the big picture, and try another path."

Dr. Snyder goes on to say that hopeful people understand that life is not fair, that there are inevitable ups and downs, and that some people have more troubles than others. They don't blame themselves for what is not their fault, nor do they feel that they are somehow being picked on by the powers that be.

Another researcher, psychologist Timothy Elliott, who is on the faculty of Virginia Commonwealth University in Richmond, uncovered similar findings. He studied people who had been paralyzed in the prime of life with spinal-cord injuries, and found that the hopeful patients had more mobility, less incidence of depression, and more friends than those who couldn't find new ways to give life value. "Hope lends a sense of existential meaning to what you do," Dr. Elliott believes. "In my studies of people with acquired disabilities, I find that many of them speak of their injury as a turning point that gave them new strength, a sense of being special, and a more profound way of leading their lives. They believe the injury occurred for a reason, and that there is something they are supposed to do as a result, such as helping other people understand how precious life really is."

This is not just surface advice about "putting on a happy face." These people have suffered terrible losses, and they have come through psychologically and spiritually whole. There is a lesson for all of us here.

Dr. Snyder agrees and adds, "Human beings are goal-oriented creatures. Over the centuries, we have proved ourselves to be marvelously adaptive as a species. Animals, when faced with what seems to be a hopeless situation, will simply lie down and die. They can't see beyond the moment, or make plans for the future. But people don't have to give up. They can find something new to live for."

Look at it this way: When a racehorse breaks a leg, there's nothing left for her, and the people who care about her shoot her to put her out of her misery. But when an athlete suffers a career-ending injury—or even simply ages out of the sport—he becomes a spokesperson for cereal or, better yet, a coach for the new generation.

You, too, can be a coach for the new generation—a spiritual coach for your grandchildren. Even if now or someday in the future your hands become too stiff to roll out a piecrust or cast a fly rod, even if you're bedridden, even if you're in many physical ways "just not what you used to be," you are still you, with an enormous amount of valuable love, knowledge, and insight to give. Actually, why would you want to be "what you used to be"? How much better to revel in the newness of what you are now and what you are still becoming—a being of

by setting a fine example, and also by making sure they know the line between their own rights and the rights of others. Again, they are far more likely to accept this important lesson from you than from anyone else in their lives.

2. ATTACHMENT
Let your grandchildren know, through words and deeds, that the bond of affection which attaches the two of you to one another can never be broken. Show them also that there is just such a bond between you and their parents. These bonds give the child a sense of security and peace. The bonds are infinitely flexible and elastic, keeping you together no matter where you are in time and space— and they endure even beyond death. Give your grandchildren this kind of assurance of safety in your constant affection, and they will grow up with a feeling of never having been alone or abandoned in spirit. They will also achieve a healthy capacity for intimacy and a willingness to be contributing members of the human race.

3. COMMITMENT
Let your grandchild know that a pledge to carry through on a promised course of action, or to stand by another person, must be honored. If your grandson says he'll play on the soccer team, he must arrange to show up for practice and scheduled games, even if that means giving up other activities such as parties or even family outings. Words like responsibility, duty, and obligation are not stuffy or outmoded. People who honor their commitments are seen by others as being moral and therefore trustworthy, dependable, and possessed of good judgment. A caveat, however: Make sure the child also

knows that while following through is commendable, he
need not continue in a situation that is unjust. Sticking
to it against all odds is just plain foolish if the other guy
isn't playing fair. Encourage the child to talk openly with
you if he ever has doubts about the right course of behavior for any given scenario. Girls in particular are still
socialized to comply at their own expense. There is a
difference between being responsible and being taken advantage of. You can help your grandchild see that difference. Encourage loyalty, faithfulness, and devotion,
but also encourage a strong sense of self-esteem and trust
in one's instincts.

4. COMMUNITY

Help your grandchild understand that no man is an island, and that sharing in a sense of fellowship with family, neighbors, and society as a whole affords us with a
feeling of belonging. As Hillary Rodham Clinton pointed
out in a speech in 1993, America suffers "from a sleeping
sickness." She went on to say that "we lack at some core
level meaning in our individual lives, and meaning collectively, that sense that our lives are part of some greater
effort, that we are connected to one another." Other researchers and thinkers have recently echoed that same
cry, among them Stephen L. Carter in his courageous
new book *The Culture of Disbelief,* and Amitai Etzioni
in his most recent work, *The Spirit of Community.* Also,
in a recent column which refers to all of these works,
award-winning journalist Anna Quindlen sums up the
problem by saying: "There is a yawning hole in the psyche of America and Americans where our sense of common purpose, of community and connection, of hope
and spiritual satisfaction should be. . . . And the discus-

sion must continue, of what morality and community mean . . . of how we will fill the vacuum."

Grandparents can go a long way toward filling that vacuum by instilling in their grandchildren a sense of the importance of community. There is nothing old-fashioned about this aspect of human life, even though the social upheaval of the last few decades has served to make it seem so. Let's move far past the "me-decade" values so that the grandchildren will have the spiritual tools to rebuild what was torn down. You can also move beyond your own family in this regard by getting involved in the burgeoning intergenerational movement which seeks to reverse the damages of our artificially age-segregated society. For further information, see the section in chapter 6 which deals with this exciting development.

5. ETHICS

From the Greek word *ethos,* meaning character, ethics are the principles of proper moral conduct. Help your grandchild grow through the stages of moral development from wanting to do right just to avoid punishment, to wanting to do right to please other people, to wanting to do right *because it is right.* The late Abraham Maslow, in his groundbreaking work *Toward a Psychology of Being,* wrote with great excitement about the discovery that human nature is essentially good and that all we need do is encourage its growth. Maslow says that unlike the instincts of other animals, human nature is not strong and overriding, but delicate and underlying. If it is not tended, it won't wither altogether, but it definitely won't flourish. We have to help it along. That's where you come in. Your grandchildren will respond eagerly to your lessons in goodness, because it's in their nature to be good. Leave the day-to-day, nitty-gritty aspects of child rearing to the parents. Yours is the domain of the inner grandchild. As always, he or she will heed you without question. Your lessons will be even more effective, however, if you give the child concrete examples. Perhaps the two of you can volunteer in the church soup kitchen, or help make Thanksgiving baskets for the needy, or wrap used toys to donate to an orphanage. Encourage your grandchildren to act in ways that expand their capacity for simple human kindness. The wonderful feeling that results is its own reward and will act as an incentive for the children to continue to do good works.

6. HONESTY

When you were still a member of the middle generation, you may have been so pressured by financial concerns that you were forced to make some compromises against your will, perhaps taking a job you didn't entirely believe in or acting as a yes-man to a boss when you wanted to say no. One woman recalls writing advertising slogans for cigarettes even though she knew it was wrong. "I felt like I was selling my soul," she says. "It was a kind of prostitution. But I was a single mother with three children and the pay was terrific. Now, thank God, I don't have to live a lie anymore. I can hang on to my values and be totally honest with my grandchildren in a way that I couldn't be with my own kids. This is such a relief!"

Like this woman, you can have another chance, a time to be true to yourself and to your grandchildren. There is no greater gift you can give them than an understanding of the importance of truthfulness and integrity. Psychologist Karen Horney had a theory that when we do something that is deceitful it "registers," and when we do something sincere, that "registers" as well. We have a kind of internal balance sheet and we become increasingly uncomfortable if the register tilts toward fraud and away from honesty. So introduce your child to the importance of truth, and just as with unacceptable physical behavior, be firm and no-nonsense in your reproval for lying or sneaking around. Let the child know that this is absolutely not allowed. Trust me, he will not turn against you. He will instead be relieved and grateful that you have helped him to balance the register.

7. Joy
Ecstatic happiness and pleasure are part and parcel of the spiritual connection between grandparents and grandchildren. Revel in this unbounded jubilance. You'll both feel better for it. Indeed, the energizing effects of joy and mirth have been documented by Dr. William Fry of Stanford University in Palo Alto, California. He demonstrated that laughter increases such vital functions as respiratory activity, oxygen exchange, muscular activity, blood pressure, and heart rate, and that, like physical exercise, laughter acts as a natural pain reliever by engaging the endorphins, the body's "inner opiates." In other words, laughter really is the best medicine. Make sure that both you and your grandchildren get generous doses.

8. Love
It is difficult to define love, that deepest and tenderest feeling of human affection. Yet as we have seen, grandparents and grandchildren share a love like no other, one

that psychology calls "unconditional positive regard." Time and again in my private practice, I saw grandparents who went on and on about their marvelous grandchildren, even though these were troubled youngsters with a variety of emotional and behavioral problems. Yet the grandparents loved the children "no matter what," as one grandfather said. This is powerful stuff. Lavish that special brand of love on your grandchildren and drink in the love that pours back to you from the children. Let nothing stop you in this regard, for this love is elemental and essential to your spirit and theirs.

9. RESPECT

Instill in your grandchildren a willingness to show esteem and consideration for others, for their opinions, their point of view, their accumulated life experience. This kind of respect also encompasses tolerance, in which the beliefs or practices of others are not prejudged or defiled. As we strive to heal a wounded world, be sure to endow your grandchild with an open mind and heart.

Do this by setting a good example in the way you treat others. Don't act superior. Don't yell at people when you're driving. Be courteous and patient with salesclerks and taxi drivers. Show understanding, compassion, and forgiveness for the plight of other people. Get rid of negative thinking and judgmental pronouncements. Put yourself in other people's shoes, and help your grandchild to do the same. For example, if you are together in a supermarket and someone behaves rudely, perhaps by cutting ahead in the checkout line and speaking curtly to the cashier, talk to your grandchild about the scene later on in private. Ask the child why he thinks the person was acting like that. Was he a bad person? Or did he have some problems that he couldn't cope with? Was he worried about something? By asking questions such as these, you are priming the child to give people the benefit of the doubt and to appreciate his own situation in life.

10. Reverence

Finally, encourage your grandchildren to experience a sense of the sacred. Foster a feeling of profound awe and veneration for the natural world, the environment, and a higher power, whatever that may mean to you and yours. Since grandparents and grandchildren like to talk about such things as nature and magic, and because children are nearer the beginning and you are nearer the end of life than the parents, it's natural for you to want to share your spiritual beliefs with your grandchildren. As people get older, they become more spiritually intelligent. Whether or not they have been religious during the middle years, they are now able effectively to use religious practices to enhance their lives. Full recognition of this is one of the most powerful coping mechanisms people have in later life. Yet children also have a natural sense of reverence. One woman who grew up to be a nun tells me that she knew God existed when she was a little girl of six or seven. She remembers looking down at a colony of ants one summer day and realizing that they couldn't see her because she was too big. Later, as twilight deepened and before her mother called her in from the backyard, she looked up at the stars and understood that God was present. He was just too big for her to see.

Unfortunately, however, while grandparents and grandchildren are spiritually aware, the parents are often out of the loop. They are consumed by the demands of life, and secular concerns push religion out of their consciousness.

This is surely why one of the complaints I hear most frequently is that grandchildren are not getting proper religious training. Grandparents usually find it a great source of joy to inculcate in a child the family's traditions and beliefs. And most of the time it's a pleasant experience. But it can be a problem if you hold beliefs that are different from those of your own children—and nowadays it's not uncommon for members of the same family to have totally different, even opposing religious views.

Do you share religious beliefs with your children? If you don't, your children may object when you try to teach your own views to your grandchildren. I have seen families break up over this issue. On the other hand, when families are loving and committed to one another, they can overcome their religious differences.

If this is your situation, sit down together and identify your differences, finding common ground and working out a compromise solution. As a general rule of thumb, remember that while you should certainly be allowed to discuss aspects of your beliefs with your grandchildren, you shouldn't indoctrinate your grandchildren contrary to their parents' wishes. And no matter what your religious differences may be, you shouldn't make the mistake of severing any relationships because of them. You and your grandchildren will suffer the most. It is important for everyone to keep in mind that the more a child knows, the better. And the greater the variety of what a child knows, the better. For the child to see that both parents and grandparents share a common belief on some level—in God, for example—even though their religions differ, is often positive enough. How a belief is expressed is secondary to a child.

Adam is a Jewish grandfather who faced this problem and, with some help, found a way to work out a unique solution. His son married Elizabeth, a devout Catholic, and promised to raise the children in the Catholic faith. Although Adam and Elizabeth liked one another very much, Adam was upset that his granddaughter Julie wasn't getting any, in his words, "Jewish education."

"I want Julie to know about my side of the family. We lost three-quarters of the family in the Holocaust. I want her to know that, but Elizabeth is against this."

Elizabeth said, "I know how Poppa Adam feels but I don't want Julie confused about who she is."

Since they were both active in their congregations, they decided to talk things over with their spiritual leaders. Adam spoke to his rabbi, Simeon, and Elizabeth to her priest, Father Pete, whom she described as a "screaming liberal clergyman." The rabbi and the priest were on friendly terms and respected one another as a result of their joint involvement in many community projects. At Adam's request, a meeting was arranged between Adam, Elizabeth, Father Pete, and Rabbi Simeon.

Rabbi Simeon pointed out to Elizabeth that Jesus Christ was, after all, a Jew, and Father Pete said to Elizabeth that Judaism can be viewed historically as "pre-Catholicism," so therefore it would be fine for Julie to learn what her grandfather wanted to teach her. Rabbi Simeon then urged Adam to attend church with Julie and Elizabeth in order to "see what happened after the Old Testament." In fact, as a result of their discussion, Adam, Elizabeth, Rabbi Simeon, and Father Pete decided to run a joint Old Testament Bible class for both congregations. Most important, everyone was happy with the way things worked out.

These, then, are the ten aspects of the spiritual connection which you can pass on to your grandchildren. As you do so, you will experience a miraculous phenomenon: You will realize that the conduit between you and your grandchildren is a two-way channel which instantaneously transmits back to you from your grandchild the beauty of her budding soul. To paraphrase the Bible: "Give and ye shall receive." Herein lies the power of the spiritual aspect of your relationship. It not only enhances the child, but it sustains *you* as well—and gives you the will to live and grow each day, each moment, as fully as possible.

Do you recall the woman we met at the beginning of this chapter, the widowed piano teacher whose arthritis kept her from continuing her beloved profession, and who had very little contact with her children and grandchildren? She had all but lost that essential will to go on. But she was saved from despair when just one of her grandchildren began to reach out to her. Darla was ten years old and an only child. She lived all the way across the country in Seattle, and had seen her grandmother only five times in her whole life. Yet when she heard that her grandmother was in the hospital with pneumonia, Darla was moved to send a handmade greeting card. The grandmother was so touched that she phoned the child to thank her. Thus began a mutually nourishing and rapturous relationship. Darla's next message of love was a handmade birthday card. Grandma, who had recovered from the pneumonia, reciprocated with a tape for Darla of her grandparents playing a Mozart sonata. They also started calling one another on a regular basis.

"That child has literally brought me back to life," the woman says. "She doesn't care if I'm old and arthritic. She doesn't care whether or not I can play the piano anymore. She just loves me. I still don't quite understand it. The love is so pure, so natural. I wonder now why I didn't keep up more with my family until Darla got things going. I guess I thought I'd be a burden and a bore. I didn't think they'd want anything to do with an old lady like me. But after Darla showed me the way, I got up the nerve to contact my other grandchildren. Pretty soon they were sending me stuff—pictures, video-tapes, drawings. And somehow, everything is better be-tween me and my own children now. They're making much more of an effort to visit. It would be nice if we all lived closer, but I see now that you don't have to let family ties go just because you're miles apart. Please put that in your book. Tell people not to shut themselves off from their families. I did for a while, and I lost my whole sense of purpose. Now I'm full of pep, always thinking up new ways to connect with my children—and most of all my grandchildren.

"Oh yes, here's the best news! Darla's twelve now and she's a good little musician, a cellist. She's coming to New York for Christmas all by herself to stay with me, and we're going to go to concerts at Carnegie Hall. She didn't even start her music lessons until after I had sent some tapes of her grandpa and me playing. She was born with the gift, certainly. But the desire—well, I like to think I had something to with that.

"Still, it's more than just the music. We share some-

thing we don't even have to talk about. It's a feeling—
that's the best I can do to explain it. There are things
you can't get across with words. Something goes on between Darla and me that's on another plane."

What this woman is talking about, of course, is the
spiritual connection. But as we have seen, grandparents
and grandchildren who live far from one another are in
danger of missing out on the miracle unless they make
every effort to stay in touch. This is one of the most
important challenges any grandparent can face. Try
everything within your power to overcome the problem
of not being available in person for your grandchildren
on a regular basis. True, your vital connection is a spiritual one which knows no bounds, but you must call
upon all of your ingenuity and spare nothing in order to
keep the connection alive across the miles.

PART TWO

The How-to's of Grandparenting Today

5

Over the River and Through the Woods

One concerned grandmother said to me after a speech I had given on the importance of the vital connection, "How can I be a good grandmother when my daughter and her family live thousands of miles away? I had always pictured myself being a regular part of my grandchildren's lives, just the way my grandma was. She lived only a few blocks away, and I used to go to her house after school almost every day. She'd bake cookies and tell these wonderful stories and give me little surprise presents. She taught me how to crochet and how to separate an egg white from a yolk. She hugged me a lot and told me I was the prettiest,

*smartest little girl in the world. I loved her so much! But
now that I have grandchildren of my own, all I can do
is talk to them on the phone and see them at Christmas.
I can't help feeling we're all missing something very, very
important."*

Once upon a time, Grandmother and Grandfather's
house really was just over the river and through the
woods. Yet today, like this woman and her grandchildren, many families are miles apart. However, even as I
acknowledge that reality, I strongly believe you should
make every effort to remedy such a situation in your own
family if there is any way at all to do so. This chapter is
designed to teach grandparents and grandchildren how
to maintain the vital connection in spite of whatever distance is between them, but the *ideal* situation is for the
elder and younger generations to be near enough for frequent person-to-person contact. That being so, I urge
you to resist the clever sales pitches of the myriad retirement communities which have proliferated in recent
years. Is a sunny climate really a good trade-off for closeness with your family? Would you honestly rather play
shuffleboard with a lot of other displaced grandparents
than play ball with your grandkids? The choice is yours,
but think long and hard before you make it. The exodus
of many grandparents to warmer locales has meant that
a substantial number of families are not getting the stabilizing benefits of having the elder generation on the
scene. As I said, long-distance grandparenting can be effective with the right strategies, but what a shame to create a gulf between you and yours through self-imposed

exile if you don't really want to abdicate your position as the resident elders in the family. In fact, a recent survey conducted by the American Association of Retired Persons revealed that of people over the age of fifty-five, a whopping 84 percent said they would prefer to remain in their own home and not move to a retirement home or community.

Strive for a sense of balance. Yes, you have worked hard and you deserve a break—but not a permanent one. The fact is that you're a parent forever, even after your children have grown up. They still need you very much. Don't relinquish your place as head and heart of the family just so that you can live an endless summer with no more reason to get up in the morning than to sun yourself or play cards with other people who are also amputated from their families.

When I spoke with one grandmother at a conference not long ago, she shook her head and said, "We retired to this lovely place in Florida three years ago. I have eight grandchildren and now I only see them a couple of times a year. I find myself wondering, 'Is this what I want, to be a grandparent who is not involved with her grandchildren?' When I think back, I see that we moved just as a kind of a knee-jerk response. We could afford it, and the winters back in Wisconsin really are brutal. But we never talked about all the consequences of moving. Actually, I just assumed my husband wanted to move and I figured I'd go along with his wishes. I mean, the man worked long and hard and he deserves a nice retirement. But I finally brought this up a couple of months ago, because I was missing the kids so much, and he told me he had thought *I* was the one who wanted to move!"

Don't let this type of communication breakdown propel you toward a leisure lifestyle if you would prefer to remain an integral and active force in the life of your family. On the other hand, even if you do choose to stay near your grandchildren, the middle generation may opt to relocate in order to find better jobs, thus making you long-distance grandparents whether you like it or not. Here again, though, with a little creative planning and a family powwow or two, you may be able to keep the whole tribe together. Two grandparents I know, Ward and Betty, held an emotional family meeting several years ago with their three children. They told them that they loved them very much and expressed their wish that they could live near one another, preferably in their hometown, once the children settled down. Betty said, "It breaks my heart to have you move away after we've loved you so much and raised you all these years."

Their children were touched by this, especially since they all got along very well. Myra, the oldest daughter, said, "I thought it was a lovely sentiment that Mom and Dad expressed, wanting all of us to be together. But I wasn't sure how practical it was. Good jobs are hard to come by."

Myra's words proved to be prophetic. Two years later her husband, Ned, was laid off from his job at a nearby auto plant. Their only option was to move away from the family in order to find a comparable job. But Ned and Myra didn't want to move away from their home.

Another family conference was held. Together, parents and grown children hammered out a solution. At first, Betty said she would be glad to postpone retirement from her job as a legal secretary—which, fortunately, was an option at her company—so that she could lend Myra and

Ned money until the plant started hiring again. But then Ward, already retired from his engineering job, offered another idea. He said he would open a consulting firm and employ Ned and Myra. Betty got very enthusiastic about that, and said she would contribute the venture capital. The firm became very successful, and the family was able to stay together.

Nevertheless, some families will be separated by many miles in spite of everyone's good intentions. Even so, you can still be a major influence in your grandchildren's lives. What is important is the consistency and reliability of your connection. The children will flourish if they know they can count on hearing from you and seeing you, even infrequently, but on a predictable basis. In fact, there is one aspect about long-distance grandparenting that is quite positive. Your visits, when you do manage to get together, will be intensely meaningful and exciting for everyone concerned. There is a certain romance to looking forward to being with those you love, plus a heightened sense of how special you are to each other. There is also, to be sure, the fresh grief that comes with saying good-bye at the end of each visit, but even that, as life experiences go, is more positive than negative. It underscores how much you care about each other.

One woman, now a grandmother herself, told me about her memories of waiting for her grandparents to come for Christmas:

> "My grandparents used to drive from Ohio to Illinois to visit us, so we were never sure exactly when they'd arrive. My older sister, Ginny, and I could hardly stand the suspense. It was awful, but it was kind of delicious at the same time. On

the day they were supposed to come, we'd all hurry around with the preparations, getting out the good china and silver, making up the beds in the den with fresh sheets, hanging up clean towels. And there would be the wonderful smells from the kitchen, because our mom always pulled out all the stops when it came to cooking for the big get-together. Anyway, about an hour before the estimated time of arrival, my sister and I would station ourselves at the side of the bay window in the living room right next to the Christmas tree. The scent, up so close, was intoxicating and to this day, a whiff of pine brings back the whole scene as if it were yesterday. Ginny and I would draw faces in the fog on the windowpanes to pass the time, and every now and then we'd think we heard a car coming and we'd press our noses against the icy glass to get a better look. After a while, the waiting got to be a kind of exquisite agony. My mother used to call to us and say, 'For heaven's sake, girls, they won't be here for at least another half an hour. Why don't you go to your room and play?' But we wouldn't budge. It was almost as though we were summoning them. It was magic. We couldn't leave our post or the spell would be broken.

"And then, at long last, the blue Chevy would turn the corner onto our street and we would start screaming, 'They're here! They're here!' We'd race to the door and run out without our coats, and they would scoop us up, with all of us hugging and laughing and crying. Grandma had a Persian lamb coat, and she'd always take it off and wrap the two of us in it and say, 'Land sakes, you'll catch your death of cold!' The coat smelled of fur and Grandma's perfume and I felt as though Ginny and I were in a special place, our secret place, better than any place in the world. You know, I still have that memory so I still have that secret place to go to when I need to feel beloved and safe.''

Intimate contact, even for a short period of time, can go a long way toward establishing a close grandparent/grandchild relationship—one which will endure for the lifetime of the grandchild, long after the death of the beloved grandparents. This point has been made clear to me during the Grandparent/Grandchild Camp my wife Carol and I hold every summer in New York's Adirondack Mountains. The grandparents and grandchildren who attend—and some live thousands of miles apart during the year—become infinitely closer during their time at the camp, and they report that they are able to hold on to this intimacy throughout the year in a much more powerful way than they had before the camp experience. One woman wrote me a heartfelt letter saying that the week her husband spent at the camp with their young grandson had changed all of their lives. "He wasn't much of a grandpa before that," she wrote. "It was the one-on-one time that did the trick. I'll never be able to thank you enough."

That so much bonding could happen within just one week may seem extraordinary, but this happens because children expand time. All of us know how long it took to grow up and how fast time passes as we age. So a little time exclusively with you can go a long way for the children, and for you as well. But the time really needs to be just for you and your grandchild.

To make sure you get this kind of time with your grandchildren, have a family meeting and brainstorm to decide how to work things out. Can you pool family resources to pay for travel? Will the parents allow children to travel alone? At what age? Also, remember to call to find out current airline and train regulations regarding the age youngsters can travel solo.

And while you're at it, ask about senior discounts, both for airfare and train fare. If you're over sixty-five, you can take advantage of special yearly deals offered by several companies. However, you've got to be willing to put up at least a thousand dollars up front, and you've got to accept certain restrictions, such as not being able to travel on weekends. Remember, however, that there may be better discounts available that do not involve sixty-five-and-over plans. Whenever you are planning a trip, make sure to inquire about all discount plans before settling on any of the above.

You might also consider traveling *with* your grandchildren rather than just visiting one another's homes. This option is becoming increasingly popular.

But whether you visit back and forth or take a trip together with your grandchildren, consider cutting costs by going off-season whenever that is feasible. Skip the major holidays, when discounts are almost never in effect, and plan instead to share family birthdays, or simply to get together for no special reason except that you love one another. Naturally, you'll commemorate the big holidays, and connect via the telephone and mails on those days, but the idea of seeing each other when you're not so rushed and expectations are not so high does have an appeal. "My grandchildren love the idea that I come to visit simply because I want to see them, and not just because it's some obligatory family holiday," says one grandmother. "I usually go in June, just after their school is out and before they leave for camp. My daughter and her husband stay home for the first couple of days, so we can catch up, and then they get away for a few days on their own. That way, we have some time all together, but the parents also get some time off, and the grandchildren and I have the house all to ourselves for a while. Johnny, the seven-year-old, started calling it 'Grandma Week,' and now we all call it that. It's our own holiday, and we're so relaxed. The weather is beautiful, and I honestly don't like flying in December anymore. So this has been our perfect solution."

Obviously, then, finding a way to spend uninterrupted time with your grandchildren is essential in maintaining the vital connection. But perhaps even more important is keeping in touch during the months you're far apart. Here are some ways you can accomplish that goal.

Telephone Visits

Your vital connection can be energized and nurtured by frequent phone communication. To avoid seeming intrusive, talk over with the parents your plans to call often, and agree on mutually convenient days and times.

"My mother-in-law used to call at five every other evening," says one young mother. "I could understand how much she wanted to know how the kids were doing, but five o'clock is insanity time with little ones. The baby would be screaming for a feeding, and my three-year-old would be starving, too, so there was all this wailing and whining in the background. Couldn't my mother-in-law figure that out? I wasn't about to hang up on her, but I just got so annoyed with the whole thing. Well, finally one day I said, 'Couldn't you call in the morning, like right after *Sesame Street* or something? That'd be a much better time for us.' So she pointed out that she can't exactly call from her office. In the end, we settled on early morning, when the rates are cheaper anyway. Why we didn't talk about this sooner, I'll never know, but at least we eventually found a solution."

This family is an example of how communication can keep the connection working—and they also found a way to minimize the expense of long-distance calls. To that end, you should find out about special rates for frequent calls to a certain area code, and shop around for the most cost-effective long-distance carrier for your needs. Telephone contact is truly the next-best thing to visiting in person. Even little babies will listen to your cooing and clucking and get to know your voice. And for older children, the idea of receiving a personal call from you is very important. Also, encourage the children to call you, having them reverse the charges. One grandfather suggests giving your long-distance calling card number to the grandchildren, with the stipulation that they use it only for calls to you.

And remember that while it's fun and important to speak to one another when something special happens—when a child gets an A on a report card or a part in the school play—it is equally important to call for no special reason other than to chat. The sound of your voice is reassuring and helps keep you "real" in your grandchild's mind. Of course, if you can afford the new videophones, so much the better. You and your grandchild can see each other's facial expressions and body lanugage as well as hear one another's voices. A videophone visit is about as close as you can get to a real one.

Video Visits

Even if you can't afford videophones, however, you may be able to treat yourselves to a video camera and a videocassette recorder (VCR). People who exchange videos rave about how much fun this is, and there is the added benefit of having a permanent record of the children as they grow. The following essay is a touching testimony to the joys of video visits:

Watching Grandchildren Grow
by Sarajene Giere

Here she is, all 20 pounds of her, strutting across the living-room floor, a pint-sized John Wayne. She's twelve months old and she's starting to walk. Forget hands and knees, it's on to the big time. She's panting, she's so excited. Her eyes are fixed on her goal—that fat green velvety sofa she likes to bury her face in.

"Come to Mommy, Elizabeth."

The baby sees her daddy's shoe lying by the sofa and plops down right there to taste it.

Here's our tracker again. The shoe has disappeared and someone has turned her around and set her within the video camera's range. Her mother beckons her to come, and this time the obstacles in her path have been swept away. Elizabeth chugs ahead, rocking side to side and paddling the air to keep her balance, homing in on the big black box on the other side of the room like a missile on a target. Nothing will stop her now.

We all had to learn to walk once. I can't remember my daughter's first steps, or how many shoes got in her way. That was twenty-five years ago.

She did so many memorable things for the second and third acts—connecting words into sentences, eating with a knife and fork, reading her first ABC book—that the act of walking was soon taken for granted. I kept a small camera in the drawer for special occasions, and I wrote down the milestones in her baby book.

Two reels of super 8mm film gathered dust in our closet for twelve years. We took home movies for a while, reluctantly. The camera had been a gift and it soon got in the way of our fun, the bright lights becoming a nuisance to manipulate. We only watched the movies when relatives visited, or when understanding friends we hadn't seen in a long time came over. Recently, I had those old rolls of super 8 transformed into videotape.

My daughter was eight years old in those silent, unfocused movies. It was a delightful experience to see the past fly by, my miniskirts and long hair, my husband's bell-bottom trousers, my daughter with her favorite cat, Frisky, and those three sharp-clawed kittens. Born in the dirty clothes pile, those three little kittens entered the world in front of an audience, rescuing me from those nagging "Mommy, where do I come from?" questions.

Lately, I can't seem to get enough of the last videotape my daughter sent. In this medium, nobody squints because of the bright lights and every detail is in perfect focus. I can hear the bird chirping from the kitchen, the telephone ringing, even the fire engine tearing down the street.

My daughter and her husband are used to providing me slices of life via video by this time. They were married on video, took the camera with them to the Grand Canyon on their honeymoon, and into the maternity ward, one year ago when Elizabeth was born.

This latest Academy Award winner was taken over a three-week period, a quantum leap in a year-old's calendar of accomplishments: the three-minute-mile power crawl; the lock-kneed "I'll stand up, won't sit down under any circumstances" position; the walk along the couch; the jaunt off on her own; the inspection of a new pair of white lace-up shoes; the trip to the petting zoo.

This chronicle has taken the place of my food fix after work, my early-morning radio talk show during breakfast, and my cup of cocoa at 3:30 A.M.

Roll 'em: My daughter wants me to hear the baby's first words. She wants to show me how smart she is, but getting Elizabeth to perform on camera is difficult. For some reason, her vocabulary disappears when Mother asks for it.

Daddy steps in with an old standby. "Toot your flute," he says, smiling proudly.

The fat little fingers poise flute to lips. "Toot, toot."

Her parents cheer.

As I stand at the kitchen table in my stocking feet, surrounded by grocery bags and the morning's leftover dishes, my dog jumps up to say hello. She's been waiting all day for me to come home from work so she can be let outside. I pick up the remote control. "Click."

"Elizabeth, toot your flute for Grandma."

Videos not only allow long-distance grandparents to experience the highlights of grandchildren's lives, but also have the added advantage of being available for instant replay whenever your heart desires.

By the same token, if you videotape yourselves—telling stories, sharing family anecdotes, baking a cake, building a fire, gardening, or whatever—you will not only give your grandchildren the chance to "visit" with you whenever they choose, but you will also be creating a priceless family archive.

Audio Visits

Another even more affordable way of keeping in touch is to make audiocassette recordings—and here again, you'll be deriving the dual benefit of exchanging current news while simultaneously creating an oral library for the future. One young family I know turns the tape recorder on at dinner, and since they do this often, everyone eventually forgets about the machine and acts naturally. "We get some great scenes to send to my parents," says the mother. "The kids are spilling milk, I'm telling them to eat their vegetables, all the normal stuff. It's so funny, and so ordinary, but that's what makes it so terrific. My folks feel like they've really been with us, and not in some artificial way. And there are wonderful moments, too, with the kids saying grace or asking kid-type questions. I'm glad we have all this preserved."

Other grandparents report that taping stories is a wonderful way to connect with grandchildren. One advocate of this practice is Clarice Orr, a pioneer in the grandparenting movement. Orr is a fifty-four-year-old grandmother from Lincoln, Nebraska, who has been teaching "grandparenting workshops" at community colleges and cooperative extensions for several years. In her classes, she presents suggestions about building better relationships with children and grandchildren, and one of her chief interests is improving relations between grandparents and their long-distance grandchildren. Mrs. Orr, proud grandmother of nine, was kind enough to share some of her personal experiences with me so I could pass them along to you. On the subject of tape recorders as a keep-in-touch tool, she says: "I often tape stories for my grandchildren. Sometimes I do it when they visit me. As we read a story together, I record it. Other times, I'll do it alone, but I talk to the child as I read the story. Personalized stories like this are really precious to the child. My grandchildren play the tapes on long car trips, for example. Even if your grandchild is nearby, the tape may come in handy for naptime or other times when you or the parents are too busy to concentrate on a story."

Another idea, contributed by the staff of Bananas and

the Project J.O.Y. programs of Creative Grandparenting, Inc., is to start a round-robin story, leaving off at a cliff-hanger moment and having the children tell the next "chapter." Then you do the next episode, and so on for a continuing saga. These experts also recommend taping yourself reading bedtime stories. They suggest that you say, "Turn the page" on the tape, and send the book as a gift so that the child can follow along almost as though you were right there.

Finally, you can sing nursery rhymes and lullabies for very young grandchildren. Don't worry if you're not quite in tune. The sweet sound of Grandma or Grandpa's crooning will delight the children and make them feel special and beloved.

Just the Fax, Ma'am!

As long as we're talking technology, let's get even more advanced. One woman told me this story: "My cousin Johnny and his brother gave their mother a fax machine for Christmas. Three of her four kids have fax machines, and three of the grown grandchildren have them. At eighty-six, she has learned to work her new machine and now faxes the grandchildren as well as the great-grand-children all the time. She loves it!"

The advantage of the facsimile machine is that you can reach people instantly, while something is on your mind. When your grandchild gets a good report card, you can have your own copy and save it for your scrapbook. You can send clippings from the paper and from magazines as well as relevant cartoons and your favorite recipes. Beyond that, you'll find that you're much more likely to jot down a bit of family news or a thought you want to share than you would if you had to compose a whole letter. Another good point: You can fax at any time without interrupting anyone, and the grandchildren can fax you back later, or give you a call when you're both free.

Of Computers, Modems, and PDA's

Another high-tech means of interacting with your grandchildren is computers. As one grandmother, now sixty-six, told me: "I never thought I was mechanically inclined, so the idea of using a computer just terrified me. But then my ten-year-old grandson bugged me until I let him teach me—and it's not hard at all! Now we each have a modem and we communicate with each other all the time. I'm so proud of myself!"

If this woman can learn, you can, too. Consider also the newest technology: Personal Digital Assistants (PDA's), which weigh less than a pound and can "learn" to recognize your handwriting. Typically, a PDA has a built-in notepad, name directory, calendar, calculator, and "To Do" list. You can fax a note, print it, or beam it with a built-in infrared transmitter to another PDA. You can also send electronic mail to most E-mail services. Talk about magic! Your grandchildren will love this way of communicating with you.

The Old-fashioned Art of Letter Writing

Even so, let's not lose sight of the fact that a good old-fashioned letter is still one of the most meaningful ways of staying in touch. Particularly when it comes to such personal messages as thank-you notes and birthday remembrances, nothing can take the place of a lovingly handwritten letter. Clarice Orr recommends beginning your correspondence with your grandchildren even before they are old enough to read. "I like to write my little grandchildren, even the ones who can't read yet," she says. "When I do, I use leftover scraps of gift wrap, and I draw hearts and X's with a felt-tip pen. I draw a smiling face with some glasses on—that's my symbol, so the toddler who can't read recognizes Grandma's sign."

Orr also takes letter writing one step further by putting together a family newsletter. "I write a weekly one-page letter, complete with headlines," she reports. "I make copies that go to all members of my far-flung family. The headlines are things like 'Matthew Gets Good Grades on Report Card,' or 'New Teeth for Jennifer.' Kids love to read about themselves, and the whole family gets news. It's not big news, but it's exciting for kids to see that Grandma thinks what they've done is great."

When you do write to young grandchildren, be sure to print so they can read what you send. You might ask for a copy of the alphabet from the child's handwriting primer to refresh your memory. Also, be sure to embellish your missives with little drawings, funny stickers, hearts, and "hugs and kisses." Children love this sort of thing.

Another tip: Create a rebus, one of those messages in which some of the words are represented by pictures. Little children just learning to read particularly enjoy these kinds of puzzles. You can make them by hand, pasting magazine cutouts in between the written words, or you can make one on your computer. Here's an example of the latter:

Dear Jennifer,

☎ miss **U**! ☎ will call **U** on the ☏ soon.

☎ am coming to your 🏠 for 🌲. We will read 📔📔, play with your 🐕 and bake a 🍽. Also, we will get to play with your new ☺ sister!

Grandma

Photographs

Grandparents are notorious for carrying pictures of their grandchildren around in their wallets, but why not turn the tables and give wallet-sized photos of yourself to the children? "I make sure my grandchildren are given a photograph of me that they can carry around," says Clarice Orr. "Too often, pictures end up on top of the TV. I try to send a photo of myself holding the telephone—that way, the little ones can visualize you when you speak on the phone."

In addition, the people at Creative Grandparenting recommend that you send photographs of yourself doing favorite activities and write stories about the pictures. Also, when your grandchildren are old enough, about five or six, give them a simple camera and encourage them to take pictures to send to you. You'll get a delightful child's-eye view of their world and of what's significant to them.

Beyond all of the above ideas, here are some special tips from the staff of Bananas and Project J.O.Y.:

For Parents and Grandchildren to Send to Grandparents:

• Create a height chart decorated with drawings and send yearly updates.

• Have each child make a collage of what grandparents mean to him or her, using magazines, cards, and photographs.

• Children can write messages on the back of homework samples.

• Frame a child's artwork for a special gift.

• Babies and toddlers can get into the act, too, by sharing prints of their hands or feet.

For Grandparents to Send to Grandchildren:

• Plant a tree in honor of a grandchild. Take pictures to show how tall it has grown. Then send a cutting so the child can grow a "twin" at the other end of the line.

- When eating in restaurants, save your paper place mats and write messages on them to your grandchildren.

- Write a message on a balloon, then deflate it for sending.

- Share your recipe for a family favorite (cookies, spaghetti sauce, etc.)—something your grandchildren and their parents like to eat.

- Find a picture of your grandchild's parent when he or she was the same age as your grandchild is now.

- Write a story about how you and your family spent the holidays when you were young, to acquaint grandchildren with ancestors they never had a chance to meet.

- Collect mementos to explain the history of your family and put together an album.

- Finally, the old tried-and-true symbol of love, send food!

Stay Abreast of Your Grandchild's World

- Television programs such as *Mr. Rogers, Sesame Street,* and *Barney* are probably a big part of your grandchildren's lives. You'll want to know who the characters are and be up on any current story lines so that you can chat about the programs knowledgeably. In addition, watching the programs affords you the opportunity to hear about many free offers. Fan clubs seek memberships; sponsors offer free coloring books; there are "official" cups and drinking glasses and, of course, a wide variety of contests. Let your grandchildren know you're thinking about them by sending in their names.

• Make a point of going to the same movies your grandchildren will be seeing, such as recent Disney releases. Naturally, you'd rather take the children, but at least if you go alone, you'll be able to talk about the films.

• A magazine that arrives every month with the grandchild's name on it is a regular reminder that Grandma or Grandpa remembers how grown-up the child is becoming. Librarians can be helpful here. They know what youngsters of a certain age are reading and what is available. At the library, you can browse through magazines to examine their content and compare them.

• Look up interesting items in print—a story about an unusual sport or personality, jokes, riddles, special comic strips—and clip them out and send them. These offerings can stretch a child's imagination, develop a sense of humor, pique new interests, and encourage reading skills.

• Play chess or some other game by mail.

• Try to find a common hobby or interest: collecting (anything), telling jokes, following sports. Think of ways to share your enthusiasm for your common interests.

Finally, take advantage of the information from the following sources:

Intergenerational Handbook

The Broome County Child Development Council of Binghamton, New York, has published the second edition of its *Intergenerational Activities Program Handbook*. The handbook, edited by another pioneer of the grandparent movement, Winifred McDuffie, and by Judith Whiteman, contains information for those interested in linking young children with the elderly. It includes essays by more than thirty professionals in the field, as well as children's artwork, photographs, detailed activity plans, and an extensive bibliography.

A Book for Long-distance Grandparents

The Long-distance Grandmother: How to Stay Close to Distant Children by Selma Wasserman, published in Point Roberts, Washington, by Hartley and Marks in 1992, is an excellent compendium of tips and true stories.

"It was from my grandmother that I learned the most important things about myself—that I was loved and therefore lovable, that I was special," says Wasserman. "Perhaps I could not have the same kind of upstairs/downstairs relationship with my grandsons that my grandparents had with me. But surely there were ways to bridge the physical distance between us, to keep the connection alive—something more than just the long-distance phone calls, Christmas parcels, and the longing for more visits."

This book is a real hands-on, nuts-and-bolts guide, full

of ideas for projects that will help long-distance grand-parents stay close to their grandchildren.

For loving grandparents and grandchildren, out of sight doesn't have to mean out of mind and absence really can make the heart grow fonder. I am keenly aware, however, that even in families with strong intergenerational connections, the vicissitudes of life in our complex society can create problems. That's why I have chosen to devote a substantial portion of the next chapter to the myriad special challenges and concerns which grandparents may face today as they strive to keep their families united and healthy.

However, I don't wish to create the impression that it is only grandparents in difficult family situations who are important—or even that elders are important only within their own families. For this reason, the following chapter also deals with the role of elders in the world at large. I believe strongly that elders have the power and the responsibility to bestow on the younger generations their accumulated knowledge and feelings, even as these continue to accrue. And you can do this not only for your own kin, but for the community as a whole.

6

The Way We Live Now

When nineteenth-century British novelist Anthony Trollope entitled one of his books The Way We Live Now, *the world was a far different place than it is today. The innate human need for emotional security in a large and loving family hasn't changed, but meeting that need has become ever more of a challenge for young and old alike. Diverse lifestyles often beget problems. But those problems can be solved. Furthermore, as part of today's elder generation, you can make a meaningful contribution to the world we live in.*

Who's Minding the Children?

Today's youngsters are the first to experience, in large numbers, day care outside the home—often followed by a latchkey childhood and, for that matter, a latchkey adolescence. The generation that is now in the teen and young adult years, born during the rebirth of American feminism, is the first to have grown up in this society with working mothers in the majority. In the past, women who worked when their children were small were either the poor underclass or mavericks who had demanding careers, or they were farm wives and mom-and-pop storekeepers who had a great deal of flexibility and extended family support. Then suddenly, from the early 1970s on, either out of necessity or desire or both, women surged into the workforce in record numbers, and most became mothers. Ironically, this development took place at a time in history when the word *family* had come to mean a two-generational unit. In other words, Grandma and Grandpa were most often not around to help out—and even if they were, many were delaying retirement or reentering the marketplace themselves.

Because working mothers—and working grandmothers—have become a fact of life in this country, we need a far better system of child care that goes long past the early years and gives school-agers and teens a safe, appealing, and productive way to lead their young lives. Otherwise, as research shows, they get hooked on TV, their first "drug," and move right along to the rampant alcohol and substance abuse we are now seeing when they are teens.

In the meantime, in your own family make it your business to help in every way that you possibly can. Have a family conference and, if you are geographically available, work out a child-care schedule in which *all* of the adults in the family have a part in caring for the child—and that includes fathers and grandfathers too. Don't be afraid of "meddling." The middle generation may well be enormously grateful for your involvement. As one young mother said: "I had no idea what it would be like to take care of a baby—let alone what it feels like to be a mother! I sailed through my pregnancy, working right up until I went into labor, and I fully intended to go back to work full-time after a six-week maternity leave. I had a day-care center all picked out, and it was a really good one. I even paid the deposit. My parents are retired and they had said they would look after the baby, but I told them I wanted to do things my way.

"Then the baby was born and everything changed. I was a wreck, sobbing about not wanting to leave the baby, and people kept saying it was just postpartum blues, but I knew it was more than that. My husband was as upset as I was. How could we leave our precious little Amy for ten hours a day in a group-care setting? I felt silly telling my parents that I had changed my mind. But you know, they were so sweet when I finally did. They never said, 'I told you so.' They just said, 'We're family. We'll work this out.' "

As it happens, the grandparents in this case watched Amy during the day until she was three years old. At that point, the parents enrolled Amy in a Montessori all-day program for two reasons: first, they felt that she was ready for a quality educational-group experience, and second, Grandma and Grandpa, due to economic necessity in these turbulent times, had come out of retirement to start a home-based mail-order business. As the mother said, "Three years old is a lot different from six weeks old. I'm thrilled with what Amy is getting at the Montessori school. She's absolutely thriving. But I'm also relieved that she had one-on-one care when she was just a baby. You have to go with your instincts."

This mother went on to say, however, that she is already worrying about what will happen when Amy starts first grade at the local public school. "Right now, she's in school until six P.M. and one of us picks her up after work. When she's in grade school—and high school, too—she'll get out at two-thirty or three. We can't afford a nanny. I'm looking into after-school programs. Or I'm hoping my parents can help again, since they work out of their home. You just keep figuring this out as you go along."

Child care in the '90s is a family problem, and you can be part of the solution. If you can help to bring up the grandchildren, do so. And if you are in a position to help the middle generation financially, do that as well. As always, have a family conference, and make sure your own children don't feel embarrassed about accepting funds from you. Even two-career couples are barely making it these days—that is a reality. So if your children are hardworking and sincere, they shouldn't let pride get in the way of allowing you to ease their burden and make life better for everyone, especially the grandchildren.

The Divorce Pandemic

For the first time in American history, a majority of marriages—55 percent as of this writing—are ending in divorce. That being so, chances are that there is at least one divorce in your family, and that your children and grandchildren have suffered its consequences.

Again, don't make the mistake of being afraid to "meddle." Whether your children are able to tell you so or not, never have they needed you as much as when they are in the throes of ending a marriage. And needless to say, your grandchildren need to know that even as their world disassembles, you are there for them with your special kind of love and caring. As one young mother said: "My husband was a loser. We tried counseling and everything, but he just wouldn't straighten out. He drank too much and he yelled at me and the kids and he could never hold a job. So the divorce was definitely a blessing. But that doesn't mean it was easy. When you get married, you believe it will work. You mean it when you say 'until death do us part.' Breaking those vows is awful. And for the children, there is so much fear. The people they thought would always be Mommy and Daddy together are now splitting up. I felt like I had to be steady as a rock for the kids, just to make sure they knew I was going to make everything all right. But I was dying inside. Thank God my mom picked up on that. She and I hadn't been all that close, but she started calling and coming over, and she even gave me some money to tide me over when I was spending so much for my divorce lawyer. Now I'm back on my feet and the kids are doing fine, but I don't know what I would have done without my mother's help. The good news is that we have a better relationship now than we ever did before. Life is funny."

As this story illustrates, grandparents have to be tuned

in to the needs of both the middle and younger generations when a divorce is taking place, and they have to
put the nurturing role into high gear, particularly if it
has been idling for a while. Noted sociologists Andrew
Cherlin and Frank Furstenberg point out that divorce
"creates both opportunities and dilemmas for grandparents. Opportunities arise from the needs parents and children have after a divorce. Grandparents, especially those
on the custodial side, can maintain or even deepen relationships with children and grandchildren by providing
material assistance, a place to live, help in child rearing,
guidance or advice."

However, be careful not to leave the "other grandparents" out of the picture. The whole family must work
together as a team to meet the challenges of divorce. As
Cherlin and Furstenberg say in *The New American
Grandparent,* "The dilemmas [after a parental divorce]
arise from the constraints imposed on grandparents, particularly on the noncustodial side, by the actions of the
middle generation." In other words, the custodial parent—most often the mother—and her parents should
make every effort to keep the children in frequent contact
with their paternal grandparents. In fact, encourage the
middle generation to have grandparent visitation rights
written into the divorce agreement in order to ensure that
the grandchildren will have the benefit of a continued
relationship with all of their elders. A recent study by
Cherlin and Furstenberg shows that when parents are
divorced, the maternal grandparents get to be with their
grandchildren more and the paternal grandparents less.
The more bitter the divorce, the greater this disparity.
As one grandmother said to me, "I used to have

a daughter-in-law. We had a wonderful relationship. Now the kids are divorced and she's become the enemy. I feel like she's holding my grandchildren hostage. She hasn't formally told me not to contact them, but I can feel the hostility whenever I call. This is just breaking my heart."

Try not to let this kind of thing happen in your family. If it is your own daughter who has custody of the children, help her to get past her feelings of bitterness and disappointment about the divorce, and encourage her to remember that the relationship between grandparents and grandchildren exists in a sphere of its own and should be respected and fostered even when—or perhaps especially when—the middle generation divorces.

Of course, there are two sides to every story. The paternal grandparents also need to be big enough to accept the situation, even if their son doesn't have custody, and to go the extra mile in order to maintain their relationship with their grandchildren. Particularly if the grandparents were a large part of the children's lives during the early years, a rift after a divorce can inflict profound psychological and emotional wounds on the children. In the words of one granddaughter, now a teenager, "What was all that about how I was the most special little girl in the world? Yeah, right. Now they don't care about me at all. They send me a birthday card and a Christmas card and that's it. Big deal. I thought I could trust them. Boy, was I ever wrong." Don't be like this young woman's grandparents. Don't betray a child's trust and love, no matter how you feel about the divorce and custody arrangements. Your grandchildren need you. That should be all that matters.

The Second Time Around

Yet if grandparenting after a middle-generation divorce is difficult, stepgrandparenting in the event of remarriage is an even bigger challenge. And these days, the likelihood of facing this challenge is great indeed. In the study by Cherlin and Furstenberg, one-third of the grandparents interviewed had at least one stepgrandchild. And while most people acquire stepgrandchildren when the middle generation remarries, others also have stepgrandchildren because they themselves have been divorced or widowed and then remarried. Obviously, some families must deal with both of these situations at the same time.

None of this is easy. Sociologists use the term *blended families,* but real life in a stepfamily is usually not as smooth as that phrase suggests. The Brady Bunch notwithstanding, children are seldom quick to adjust to the demands of getting to know and accept a stepparent and stepsiblings. Here again, if you are sensitive to the situation, you can be a great help to everyone involved. You already know your own grandchildren, and your emotional radar should let you pick up their distress signals. Naturally, dealing with stepgrandchildren whom you've just met is trickier. Still, the Grandparent Project has shown that if stepgrandparents go gently, and are available without asking for any reward or feedback—such as verbal declarations of the children's love and respect— the majority can develop significant attachments. Just don't try to rush things. Stepgrandparents are well advised to wait in the family wings before entering a child's life. The stepgrandchildren I interviewed were dealing with profound psychological issues such as divided loyalties, comprehending the circumstances leading to the remarriage of the child's custodial parent, working through the dissolution of the parent's marriage, and trying to make sense of a new family configuration. This is a tall order, and the last thing a child needs is to be expected to have an instant relationship with stepgrandparents. In fact, the children may even resent you at first because they see you as an extension of the other interlopers in their once secure family life.

Consequently, the watchwords for successful stepgrandparenting are patience, support, loving, caring, and being noncompetitive. Eventually, you can be a new friend and a new person to love for your stepgrandchildren. Just be careful to let your new wards come to you. Be there for them when they are ready—consistent and reliable. Remember, don't try to win them over, and certainly don't try to buy their love with gifts. They need the essence of you, and in time you will become an important person in their lives. Children have no built-in limit to the amount of people they can love. As a stepgrandparent, you extend the child's intergenerational support system, and you all benefit as a result. Effective stepgrandparenting is an art, but it can be a source of revelation, great joy, and wonder for those who undertake the role with sensitivity, tenderness, and compassion. Your relationship can blossom into that of *beloved elder/beloved child*, terms which I use to denote a deep emotional attachment between nonbiologically related elders and children.

Chosen Children

Stepgrandchildren, however, are not the only nonbiological grandchildren you may have. Your children may adopt a child, or conceive a child with the help of sperm banks, in vitro fertilization, frozen embryos, or even surrogate mothers. There are some basic principles to remember in these cases. First, your children yearned for a child so much that they went to any lengths to become parents. Their child is a wanted child if there ever was one. That is a tribute to the parents, and indirectly to you and the other grandparents. In addition, your children view the child as a gift to you, especially since they had difficulty conceiving. Therefore, it is important to be especially appreciative and supportive.

Second, your grandchild doesn't know, or care, that you are not her or his blood relative if that is the case. All you have to do is let the vital connection take over. One grandmother had a daughter who couldn't have children and adopted a Korean orphan. "I'm ashamed to say that before I saw the child, I was concerned about whether I would love her," this woman admits. "But when I first picked Kim up and she grabbed my finger and smiled at me, it was all over. My worries went down the drain. I was a grandma and I loved that baby so much! I couldn't hold back the tears. I looked at her, that little ten-month-old person who had just been airlifted all the way from Seoul, and I thought, my God, what if I had never known Kim!"

Like this grandmother, let your instincts go to work for you. And remember that you are important in your grandchild's life not only during the early years, but into adolescence as well. Adopted children in particular may have a rough time when they pass through a period of identity crisis as teenagers, and they may have fights with their parents, saying, "You're not my real mother and father anyway!" The best response to this is simply, "You are our child and we are your parents." That's comforting to the child, no matter how hard he or she tries to get rejected. Often, though, parents are so hurt and confused that they don't handle the situation well. That's when it's time for you to play a consoling, listening, supportive role. You are well positioned to do this because the grandchild views you as solid and stable figures, exempt from the Sturm und Drang of the relationship with the parents. So counsel both generations as they weather this almost inevitable phase.

Grandchildren in Nontraditional Families

Then there are the many children who live in nontraditional families: children of lesbian or gay parents, children of single mothers by choice, children raised in communes, and the more potentially dangerous situation of growing up in a cult. Youngsters in any of these situations have many issues and conflicts to resolve. This is all the more difficult when children go through a period of wanting to be the same as everyone else, around the age of six or seven and later during the teen years. At these times, you as the grandparents can be a stabilizing force, and serve as family bedrock for these youngsters. Without rendering judgment, as long as they are well cared for, you can quietly serve as a source of tradition for these children who may be frightened or embarrassed about their unusual family situation, no matter how lovingly their parents have explained their personal choices and orientation.

Therefore, if your own child is involved in a nontraditional relationship or group, and grandchildren are born, make helping all of them a priority. Spend time with everyone involved. Reserve your criticism, and simply find ways to support both the middle generation and the grandchildren as they deal with the difficulties of coping in a world that little understands the way they are living their lives.

Child Abuse:
Blowing the Whistle

According to a report published in December 1992 by the U.S. House of Representatives, there has been an increase of 147 percent in child abuse and neglect reports in the last decade, for a total of 2.4 million cases. And my research has shown that grandparents are often the first persons to realize that their grandchildren are being abused. When parents are not chronic abusers or addicts, but simply people who are overwhelmed by the demands of parenting, a friendly and loving word from you, with a genuine offer to help, can get to the bottom of the reasons that abusive practices are taking place. However, be honest with yourself. It is well documented that child abusers were often abused as children themselves. If you were not an effective parent, don't let the consequences be visited on yet another generation. You have been given a second chance. Get the entire family into therapy and make it your business to right the wrongs of the past and create a bright future for those you love so much.

In many cases today, however, the middle generation are not people who were abused, but people who have serious problems with alcohol and other drugs. These problems cut across all socioeconomic lines, and middle- and upper-middle-class families are far from exempt. Yet blowing the whistle when their own children are abusing a grandchild is a difficult, if not nearly impossible, act for many grandparents. And when grandparents do muster the courage to contact authorities, the abusing parents almost always ban the grandparents from seeing their grandchildren. When the parents' marriage is intact, there is legally nothing the grandparents can do about that, and so by trying to protect their grandchildren, they have effectively robbed them of the only safe people in their lives. This is a terrible price for everyone to pay, but when grandparents cannot change parents' behavior, the only recourse is to go to social service agencies for help. This way, you at least spare your grandchild until the parents begin to solve their problems and become effective parents once more.

Grandparents Raising Grandchildren

In extreme cases, though, you may end up raising your grandchildren, either temporarily or permanently. There are more than 4 million grandparents raising grandchildren today, and while some are doing so because the children have been orphaned, the majority are taking over for parents whose problems and addictions are preventing them from coping with child rearing.

Raising grandchildren is time-consuming and costly, but most grandparents in this situation talk about the life-giving and energizing benefits of having youngsters in their charge. Although saddened and angered by the inability of their own children to be effective parents, the grandparents say that saving the grandchildren's lives has given new meaning to their own lives. Many of those who had become sedentary with retirement now feel more alive and energetic. "I have to keep up with Sally after all," one grandmother said. Some feel literally transformed. As one grandfather noted with enthusiasm, "I've got a new lease on life."

Still, it isn't easy to reenter the world of hands-on parenting, complete with school, lessons, sports, birthday parties—and discipline. But the real problem is that grandparents who raise their grandchildren get little support for their efforts—certainly no money, and often no legal or financial recognition. Grandparents who have grandchildren living with them, and who do not have custody, may have to pay not only for the children's support but for their education too. Although the state offers financial support to parents and foster parents, it offers no such help for grandparents.

Without social status or legal custody, a grandparent's ability to assure a child a sense of continuity is difficult. In fact, many children express their deep concerns about being removed from grandparents by a parent recovering from a drug problem before the parent is truly rehabilitated. According to social worker Sylvie de Toledo, who started Grandparents As Parents, a support system in California for grandparents raising grandchildren, this revolving-door syndrome is quite common. When they are in periods of remission, addicted parents reclaim their children; then, when they go back on drugs, they abandon the youngsters again. Without legal guardianship, grandparents have no power to oppose the will of parents. Not only that, government agencies which deal with abandoned children often ignore grandparents who wish to raise their own grandchildren, and place the children in the care of a series of strangers.

That being so, should grandparents seek permanent custody? This is a perplexing question. The answer depends on one overriding factor: the potential for the parents to recover. This, of course, is a gamble, and even if the parents do make it, the process takes time. What happens to youngsters in the interim? Children need a sense of stability and continuity. Barbara Kirkland, a pioneer in the grandparent caretaker movement, feels that if parents aren't available, "arrangements should be made for children to get on with their lives—not remain in limbo. All children deserve a future of belonging." I agree with this compassionate and caring statement. But remember that parents cannot be permanently banished from the heart and mind of a child. Recognize that the child knows he or she has parents, however ineffective they may be. Hopefully, one day when the child is old enough, he or she will come to terms, in a psychological and spiritual sense, with this reality. And compassionate grandparents must be supportive in helping the youngster work through these issues.

This takes a great deal of flexibility and love on the part of grandparents, particularly if a formerly abusive parent returns rehabilitated to reclaim a place in the family. Because this may in fact happen, you are probably well advised not to have the children think of you as

parents or call you "Mom" and "Dad." However, each
family is different, and you should listen to the child and
to your own heart. One grandmother asked her granddaughter, "Should I be your grandmother acting like a
parent or should I be your mother?" Her grandchild re-
plied, "If I am your grandchild I will not have a mother
or father. And if I don't have you I don't have anybody."
When custody papers were signed she said, "Grandma,
can I go to school tomorrow and tell them I am going
to have a real mom now?" As far as this child is concerned, she needs her grandparents in this parental role.
Perhaps her feelings will change as she gets older, perhaps not. In any case, as long as her grandparents are
willing to respond to her needs, to her scripting for their
roles in her family, they will be doing the best possible
for her.

But what happens to grandparent "magic" when
grandparents act as parents? Does the child lose her
grandparents? The answer, at least to some extent, is yes.
Grandparents have to relinquish some of their grandparental prerogatives when they act as full-time parents.
After all, the magic ingredients of the grandparent/grand-
child relationship—unconditional love, playfulness,
spoiling, a loving "conspiracy" against the middle generation—are partially rooted in the grandparents' lack of
direct responsibility for their grandchild. Also, children
do instinctively want their caretaker grandparents to behave as parents, because realistically, children need limits
and guidance. Even so, in my own work I have noticed
that children raised by grandparents are less rebellious
and more understanding and thankful than children
raised by parents. That's because they are deeply grateful
for what their grandparents are doing for them.

And for their part, the grandparents are more gentle and understanding than they were as parents the first time around. "Sure, I enforce the rules," a grandfather said, "but I'm less strict and harsh than I was with my own children." And one grandmother told me that she is happy she doesn't make the same mistakes with her grandchild that she made with her own children. Her husband agreed: "I never gave my own children the time and attention I give my grandson. I wish I had my own family to raise again. I would be a much better father."

However, I don't want to minimize the concerns of grandparents who raise their grandchildren. In an excellent study of fifteen grandmothers raising grandchildren, Denise Breinig-Glunz, a social worker, discovered some of the apprehensions experienced by elderly grandparents raising grandchildren, including worrying about potential illness, about not having enough energy left to handle another crop of teenagers, and about the possibility of dying before the children have reached maturity. These women sought out other family members and support groups to help them assuage their fears. This resulted in stronger family networks and a national Grandparent Movement that has bonded these grandparents together. This movement has initiated efforts to gain legal and financial recognition and support for grandparents raising grandchildren. The lack of social recognition and support for these grandparents is disgraceful and must be corrected quickly.

I have found that grandparents who raise their grandchildren initiate a positive ripple effect in their environment. Families bond together to support them. Everyone feels good about what the grandparents are doing. Almost all of the grandparents I know in this situation feel that they are saving their grandchild, and have no reservations about what they are doing. "Not for one second," one grandfather answered when I asked him if he had any hesitation about raising his grandchildren after their parents were killed in a car crash. "It's natural to take them. That's what grandparents are for."

For me, grandparents who raise their grandchildren are heroic figures. Not only are they demonstrating their love and commitment to their families, they are showing our society the power and influence of their role. They deserve our admiration and our support.

Grandchildren's Problems

Of course, even when your own children are model parents, your grandchildren may present special challenges. One child may be born with a birth defect, another may have serious behavior or emotional disorders, and still another could prove to be learning disabled. These problems appear to be more prevalent today, but in fact they have always been around. In the past, they were often hushed up or never properly diagnosed in the first place. Facing these issues squarely may be new to you, but doing so gets you up to speed, so to speak. This is part of your grandparent education, an expansion of your being, and it's never too late to learn. You are being called upon to give concerned and overburdened parents a full measure of love and understanding. Remember, you're still a parent even though you're a grandparent, and this is another chance to be the best parent you can. Get acquainted with your grandchild's difficulties and learn about the nature of and solution for these problems. Visit with the doctors or other experts and ask questions. Visit the library, and read about the problem. If there is a group or publication concerned with your grandchild's problem, subscribe to the publication and join the group. In short, become an expert.

Having a grandchild with a disability is stressful but also offers an opportunity for a loving grandparent to really make a difference in the lives of hurting parents, and in the life of the grandchild. I realize, of course, that the initial shock is tremendous, whether the disability is congenital or acquired. Grandparents experience a grandchild as an extension of themselves projected into the future. They naturally dream of a child who will continue their beliefs, pursue higher education, surpass their own achievements, or practice a cherished profession. With the birth of a handicapped child or the establishment of a child's disability, these hopes are often dashed. Yet every child is special and in need of your love. You need to take an emotional step back and reorder your priorities. Whether your grandchild is a Down's syndrome child, a child who is blind or hearing impaired, a child with cerebral palsy, or a youngster who sustains a crippling injury, you and the parents can find the unique qualities that this young member of your family brings to the world. True, the repercussions in the family will be numerous and extensive, but never have you been more needed. Help the parents accept their new reality by drawing on understanding, compassion—and an appropriate sharing of tasks. Give your children support before their energies are seriously depleted. And if the parents are consumed by worry and care for the disabled child, you may need to point out what is best not just for the child but for all members of the family as well, particularly the other children.

Also, you may have to help parents get past a period of denial. For one thing, the first indication of a child's problem may not occur with birth and often not within the first year of the child's life. Parents may refuse to face the implications of a disability. They may feel deeply sad about the child but hide their fear and dismay by stressing the positive aspects of a child's development, in hopes that the problem is imagined or will go away, particularly if the child shows signs of developmental delay or autism. The parents may deny their own pain and frustration, yet look to the grandparents for emotional support.

It is important to view the situation in perspective. The life of a family cannot revolve solely around one child's differences. But rare are the grandparents who do not themselves experience some ambivalence and secret disappointment about the disabled grandchild. You are only human, after all. You may think you have been given a bad deal. Resentment, discomfort, and embarrassment may initially take the place of family pride. How can you, as a grandparent, overcome these feelings and learn to be a positive force? If your feelings are overwhelming, it will help for you to talk about your fears and anxieties with other people—a pediatrician, a friend, a social worker. Fear of the unknown—in the form of intimidating terminology or strange behavior in the child—can often be alleviated through the information.

Grandparents can help the parents, too. You may notice newspaper or magazine articles about special care or education programs or new sources of information about the particular problem. Parents will most certainly appreciate any new information which you bring to their attention.

And your direct relationship with the child can contribute mightily to the child's progress. The more positive stimulation for the child, the better. The three R's essential to the well-being of disabled children—repetition, relaxation, and reward—can be your special domain if you choose. You can provide the love and attention that will make these three R's work.

The personal involvement of grandparents is critical to the grandchild's well-being, and everyone involved with the child's care—from doctors to parents—needs to understand this. All children want to grow, to have freedom, and to have fun. They want an education, and they want to progress the best they can. Grandparents can be a basic, integral part of the network of resources that forms an emotionally healthy, tension-free circle of security for their children and for their children's children.

A beautiful example of this in action is a letter from the grandparents of a child with attention deficit disorder to that child's parents. Their letter was first printed in the 1990 fall/winter edition of *CHADDER*, the magazine of the parents' organization for children with this disorder. Attention deficit disorder afflicts approximately one out of twelve children, and five boys for every girl. The disorder can be present with or without hyperactivity. It is a confusing clinical syndrome to the family because the child looks fine and healthy but behaves in an impulsive way. In this situation, grandparents can offer respite and support to parents who are worn down from caring for a child who is intelligent but has trouble with concentrating, paying attention, and controlling behavior. This syndrome bewilders everyone, including the youngster. Untreated, the condition can seriously impair the child and create a great deal of marital and family turmoil.

For grandparents of children with ADD—as well as any disorder or disability—nurturing the parents and helping the grandchildren cope with problems often requires the shedding of old attitudes and behaviors. It can be a painfully slow process of education and understanding. Here is the extraordinary letter I referred to. These heartfelt words will help you understand what the grandparents of a disabled child go through as they try to understand the situation and be of some help:

Dear Kids (you are still kids to us),

This letter isn't easy to write, but here goes.

A lot has happened since our grandchild was born. We remember the worry and nervousness that go along with any birth, the fear of the birth defects, the unknown . . . then the burst of joy when everything seemed to be OK. Our expectations and hopes soared with yours, as our grandchild appeared to be free of problems and ready to thrive in this world.

We remember starting to watch you raise your child and we gave our advice generously, basing it on the wisdom we had gained from raising you . . . you turned out fine which proves that we are experts!

Then, as your child grew and started to present problems that you could not solve, despite our ever-so-helpful advice, we thought to ourselves that you must be doing something wrong. Both you, and we, his grandparents, were caught unprepared for the scenario which began to unfold before our eyes. Behavioral patterns seen only in "other families" became a very real tragedy for you and completely misunderstood by us. We muttered in the background, "If only they would . . . Whose genes . . . ? Not mine, for sure! Why do they indulge him? Nothing is wrong when he is with us! A good old-fashioned spanking . . . !"

As our advice developed an edge, we were unknowingly joining the chorus that accompanied you as you moved through your daily routines with your child. You felt blamed from all directions. People in stores glared at you as you tried, over and over, to get your child to behave. You were constantly embarrassed by being "obviously" bad at parenting, unable to put our infallible advice to use.

The next bitter pill came when you let it be known that you were seeking professional help, not only for your child, but for yourself. To us, who had based our philosophies of life upon self-reliance and religious principles, you may well have signed up with a witch doctor! We felt you were rejecting our tried-and-true ways, and were about to be exploited by false experts, who spouted mysterious labels ("oppositional"? "ADD"? "ADHD"? "LD"? "fine and gross motor delay"?) and other mumbo jumbo, who would take advantage of your gullibility, take your money . . . and do no good.

We let you know of our misgivings, but we had gotten used to your weary voices and eyes, telling us, in response to our objections, what your so-called experts were telling you.

Thank God there was enough love in our family to weather those awful times, when we actually added to your burden.

And thank God you listened to the experts!

Finally, after years of heartbreak, all that mumbo jumbo started to make sense!

Gradually, we began to see that our grandchild was not just a spoiled brat. We began to recognize patterns in his behavior which were, at last, understandable to us, based upon principles promoted by your experts. We became more familiar with the jargon, as we tentatively entered what was, for us, foreign and uncharted territory.

We, who thought we were educated, experienced, and tough, are babes in the woods compared to you, you kids, who are now able to teach us.

Now we can listen to you and hear you.

Although we have felt all along that we are in the same boat, now all of our oars are pulling in the same direction.

It is still a rugged journey, but we hope it is a little easier now that we aren't sniping at you.

So kids, please forgive us. We hope we can heal the hurt brought about by our misunderstanding of your struggle. Our hearts are filled with love and the best of intentions for you and our grandchild. We are flesh and blood. We want so much to help that we pray that our clumsy efforts can provide some measure of comfort and support for you all!

Thanks for hanging in there, until you could reach us and teach us.

One thing we have learned: you are good parents for our grandchild, the best. He needs you.

And now let us preach a little. We are lucky. We are bonded together by love, strengthened by the trials that could have fractured a less fortunate family. Thanks to that love, we have a unified family

support group that will not waiver, essential if our
grandchild is to have a solid foundation upon which
to build his life.

We will always be here for you, if you should ever
need an ear, a shoulder, or, God forbid, advice! That's
what grandparents are for!

Love,
Mom and Dad

Grieving a Grandchild's Death

Of course, all other problems pale in the face of the most
profound of human tragedies—the loss of a child. In
"The Grief of Grandparents," a booklet published by the
La Crosse Lutheran Hospital in Wisconsin, four stages
of grief are described. Understanding this process can
also be useful not only when a grandchild dies but also
when one of your adult children has an abortion. Abortion is a highly sensitive and politically charged issue, but
the fact is that even a well-thought-out abortion for a
compelling reason produces grief—often oddly mingled
with relief—not only for the middle generation but for
the elders as well. Grandparents' feelings about a child's
abortion range from compassion to hurt and anger, or
some combination of all three. Most often, their feelings
remain unspoken, however, because they don't want to
add to the turmoil of their own child. They are confused
about what to say or do when their child plans an abortion. One fifty-five-year-old woman said, "I can't help
feeling that I lost my grandchild, my flesh and blood. But
I don't want to upset my daughter. She thought she was
doing the right thing. She's young and single and she felt
she couldn't have given the child a decent life, and that

her own life would have been seriously compromised."
What this woman didn't realize was that her daughter
was in great need of love and support. The young
woman finally approached her mother for a talk, and
they stayed up until one in the morning getting all of
their feelings out. "I wish I had been more sensitive,"
says the older woman in retrospect. "My daughter made
a decision she believes is right, but she's only human. She
has feelings. We're both a lot closer now that we've
shared all this." No matter what your personal view is
on the issue of abortion, then, be there for your adult
children and don't be surprised if there is grief to be
worked through for all of you.

The first stage of grief, whatever the cause but particularly after the untimely death of a child, is shock and disbelief. In the second phase, parents yearn for the baby and
search for a reason for the loss. And they may be angry,
very angry, at doctors, friends, God, and even their own
parents. Most of all, they will be angry at themselves or one
another, trying to find a reason, and they may lay blame to
explain what happened. Grandparents may do this too.

In the third stage, parents are deeply depressed. They
may express feelings of hopelessness and helplessness. Finally, most parents will heal. But this will take time, even
several years, until the acute pain of the experience sub-
sides. The grandparents' role through all of this is one of
a guide. It is the parents who must make funeral arrangements, put away the child's things, and deal with their
memories. Grandparents must be available to respond
flexibly to the parents' needs; to provide a shoulder to
cry on, to temporarily operate the household, to deal
with friends and relatives, and to care for children.

One particularly devastating situation is sudden infant

: *Creative Estate Planning*
e Americans for the 1990s
prehensive guide to estate
man's language. Pay special
oblems of Equity Among

rtune" by Adriane Berg is
from Testamentary Press
g is an attorney as well as
r Lost Time: How to Re-
and host of New York's

egacy of Love

everything when it comes
ren, heirlooms are a piece
a book with a pressed rose,
h or newspaper clipping—
t for a moment on the po-
s and what they mean to
oom to a child, however,
to receive it. When a child
not grasp the significance
ay be careless with the gift.
very impressed with heir-
-old boy who was thrilled
y his grandfather who had
timental objects have great

u can give is a memory
atricia Pilling, an oral his-

death syndrome (SIDS)—the unexplained and unexpected death of an apparently healthy baby between the ages of one month and a year. Sometimes called "crib death," this phenomenon claims the life of approximately seven thousand infants a year. SIDS cannot be predicted or prevented, even by a physician. This tragedy can produce intense grief and pain among family members. For grandparents it is double grief. Not only is a grandchild lost, but the parents must be comforted. This leaves little time for grandparents to deal with their own sense of loss. Parents must deal with overwhelming guilt-driven depression and soul-searching because they often hold themselves responsible for the death. Grandparents must be especially supportive and noncritical during this period.

Remember that the infant victim's sisters and brother suffer too. Sometimes they don't show their grief. This is where grandparents can be particularly helpful by spending a great deal of time with the children and discussing the event when the child is ready to talk. Grandchildren should be informed that SIDS is a disease that occurs unexpectedly, is noncontagious, and won't happen to anyone else in the family. In a fact sheet on SIDS, the Sudden Infant Death Syndrome Regional Center of Eastern New York State offers the following list of "don'ts" for grandparents who have lost an infant grandchild to SIDS. These same guidelines can be applied to the death of an older child as well.

- Don't let your sense of helplessness keep you from reaching out to a bereaved parent.

- Don't avoid them because you are uncomfortable.

- Don't say you know how they feel.

- Don't say, "You ought to be feeling better by now."

- Don't tell them what they should feel or do.

- Don't try to find something positive about the child's death.

- Don't point out that at least they have other children.

- Don't say that they can always have another child.

- Don't suggest that they should be grateful that they have other children.

- Don't make any comments suggesting that the care they gave the child was inadequate.

Here are some positive things for grandparents to do.

- Let your concern and caring show.

- Say you are sorry, and that you are available.

- Allow the parents to express their grief.

- Encourage them to be patient with themselves.

- Allow them to talk about the child as much as they need to.

- Assure them that they are good parents and did the best anyone could.

- Give special attention to your other grandchildren.

- *Leaving Money Wisely* for Middle- and Upper-Incom by David W. Belin is a com planning, written in clear lay attention to chapter 4, "Pr Grandchildren."

- "Saving the Family Fo an audio course available (800-934-2211) for $29. Ber the author of *Making Up fo claim Your Wealthy Future* WABC's *Money Show*.

Heirlooms: The

Of course, money is far from to leaving a legacy. For chil of you. Whatever the object— an army medal, a photograp children will cherish it. Refle tential heirlooms you posses you. When offering an heirl make sure the child is ready is very young, he or she may of what you are doing and m School-agers, however, are looms. I recall one seven-yea when he was given a medal h won it on Iwo Jima. Also, se meaning for teenagers.

Another wonderful gift y book. The brainchild of Dr.

torian and anthropologist, a memory book can chronicle the cultural, historical, emotional, and geographic context of your life experience and become part of your family's archives. Use a cassette recorder along with visuals such as photographs and other memorabilia to create this treasure. Special attention should be paid to recalling humorous events. As for the photographs, they might show other family members, homes, schools attended, and personal milestones such as graduations, weddings, and religious events. From pictures of pulling taffy to Christmas at the turn of the century or the circus coming to town, there is no end to what could be preserved in the memory book. Documents can be included too: high school diplomas, newspaper articles, marriage certificates, letters. The process is like putting together a jigsaw puzzle. Collect your memories, feelings, thoughts, and opinions, then bind them with your name on the front and spine of the book. By producing your own memory book, you can give the people you love a way to gain a profound understanding of your life.

Grandparents' Day

A good time to present your memory book to the grandchildren is on Grandparents' Day, which falls on the second Sunday in September. This holiday was instituted in 1978 by a group of grandparents from the Midwest, and the original intention was to have people set aside a special time to celebrate the place of elders in their family and society. Unfortunately, the concept never really caught on. I must admit that I was skeptical from the beginning about the establishment of yet another holiday which would surely be commercialized. When giving gifts is an empty act of obligation, no one benefits.

Yet it's not too late to make Grandparents' Day into an event that serves an important purpose. But this can't happen if Grandparents' Day continues to be thought of as a made-up holiday with grandparents on the receiving end of store-bought gifts. Rather, a meaningful Grandparents' Day should be a day when grandparents, and great-grandparents, make a point of showing their value by giving love, time, and wisdom and sharing their life experience with their loved ones.

Grandparents' Day can offer a way for grandparents to affirm their place and their value in their families and society. A truly meaningful Grandparents' Day can be a time for grandparents to celebrate their worth, to savor their own importance, and to show it. It can be a time for grandparents to gather their families together, to talk about their lives together, to examine new options, and to heal old wounds. It can be a sorely needed time to reaffirm family connections and love. A real Grandparents' Day, therefore, is a day for the family to reflect about grandparents' place and roles. It is also a day for the community to do the same. Thus, grandparents should not be passive participants on Grandparents' Day. They should make it happen. Grandparents' Day should be an emotional and spiritual celebration that is responsive to the current form of the family, an important consideration in these times of changing family structure. It should be a day of giving of yourself, of sharing hopes, dreams, and values, of setting an example for future generations—and most of all having fun with grandchildren.

Grandparents' Day in Your Grandchildren's School

Beyond the official Grandparents' Day with your family, you might also want to do as many grandparents have already done and start a Grandparents' Day in your grandchildren's school. This is a wonderful way to get firsthand knowledge about what your grandchildren's world is like and what they are being taught, and to share your experience with the children.

Don't be hesitant to storm the walls of what may seem like an impenetrable bureaucracy to start such a program. Our experience has shown that school administrators increasingly welcome grandparents who want to create such a wonderful event. The first thing you should know is that you don't have to do it all yourself. Grandparents' Day in the School should be a community event. You'll want to rally not only grandparents, parents, and grandchildren but also local businesspeople, media, and community agencies. Once you line them up, they can do most of the work. All you have to do is lead. Here's a game plan.

PLANNING

• First, create a planning committee that includes the school principal, the head of the parents' association, and assorted community leaders. The next task is to identify a date for the event. Make sure that you allow plenty of lead time so long-distance grandparents can make arrangements to attend. This is very important.

• Next, have the principal notify the teachers about the event and encourage them to discuss it with their students and decide how they can incorporate the event into their classes. This will get their creative juices flowing. Children can invite their grandparents and ask them to teach, share experiences, tell stories, and show off their talents.

• Have the principal and the parents' association write to all of the students' families explaining the event and inviting their grandparents to participate. List activities—music, singing, storytelling—that grandparents might perform and ask grandparents to sign up for each activity.

• Plan a potluck kickoff dinner on the eve of the day for grandparents, parents, grandchildren, and appropriate community members. Invite interesting speakers and entertainers. Have the press attend.

• Set up a schedule for the day. Grandparents should attend and participate in classes. Have the day end with a barbecue and square dance. Make sure that teachers discuss the event in their classes after the fact and ask students for feedback.

ACTIVITIES

• Have a coffee and doughnut time, and a meeting room where grandparents can congregate.

• Have an assembly program with the children.

• Have an open-house time when children can give their grandparents a tour of their school.

• Grandparents can have lunch with the children.

- Have children interview their grandparents on audio- or videotape.

Grandparent Classes

Grandparent classes are a way to raise grandparents' consciousness about their roles and responsibilities. You can start one in your local church, the obstetrics ward of your hospital, or your local school or community center. An excellent curriculum for grandparenting has been conceived and published by Drs. Robert and Shirley Strom of Arizona State University in *Achieving Grandparent Potential* and *Becoming a Better Grandparent*. The curriculum and teachers' handbook may be used in a diversity of settings in order to empower grandparents to be more effective in their families and communities.

Grandparent Support Groups

Many grandparents have formed their own discussion and support groups, and you might like to do the same. Most groups center on specific issues such as grandparent visitation, grandparents raising grandchildren, and expectant grandparents. The American Self-Help Clearinghouse in Denville, New Jersey, has published a set of guidelines. The clearinghouse believes that self-help groups "offer people the opportunity to meet with others in order to share their experiences, ideas, and hopes. Run by and for their members, self-help groups might be better described as 'mutual help' groups. They are started by ordinary people who recognize that they and others like them can benefit from sharing and pooling their knowledge, understanding, and practical information."

You don't have to be an expert organizer or people manager to get a self-help group off the ground. The clearinghouse does suggest, however, that you keep a few rules of thumb in mind as you formulate your group. If you are in an area served by a self-help clearinghouse, ask a representative for any information the office can provide to help you get your group started. The office may sponsor workshops or be able to put you in touch with others who have expressed interests similar to yours. Also keep in mind that if you are concerned about a specific grandparenting issue, there may already be a national organization that can help you.

According to clearinghouse information, the next step is the most difficult. Once you have established that there is a need for a group in your area, you have to find other grandparents who are interested in helping to start, not just participate in, the self-help group. The clearinghouse recommends that you post notices at appropriate public places—the post office, the community center, the library—to generate interest. Newspapers often publish brief public-interest notices for free, or for a small fee.

Once you've found people who share your feelings and vision and are willing to help you organize the meetings, you've got your steering committee. Finding a meeting place can be a challenge, but good places to start looking include the local church, synagogue, library, senior center, or community center. Small groups might even be comfortable meeting in the home of a member. Scheduling is also a consideration. Should the group meet weekly or monthly? Where will everyone park? Will it be possible to carpool?

After the logistics have been worked out, it's time to organize the constituency. Once again, it will pay to advertise. Post flyers and notices. Local newspapers might even be willing to do a story on the formation of the group.

The agenda for the first meeting should allow enough time for you to carefully describe your intentions and feelings, and for others to do the same. The more relaxed the atmosphere, the better. In addition to a discussion of issues and topics, you might also want to address the need for future meetings and their format, activities the group might undertake, and a distinct definition of the group's purpose.

The clearinghouse also recommends that groups consider some outside activities—for example, outings with grandchildren, or hobby sharing—as well as enlisting the help of a professional consultant who would be willing to address the group on occasion to give expert advice. You might also want to organize group projects, such as the development of a promotional or informational flyer or a list of reference materials.

Reach Out and Touch Everyone

It is not only the people in your own family and immediate community who stand to gain from your legacy. You are a grandparent, but you are also an elder in this society. True, ours has become an age-segregated society instead of a tribal community. Children and adults rarely mix. Generations are segregated in attitude, in thinking, in behavior, and in geographic proximity. But you and the rest of your powerful generation can begin to reverse this regrettable development. Through sheer numbers, and with an aggregate of pride and self-esteem, you can restore the rightful role of revered elders and achieve a status which will benefit young and old alike.

Thus far in this book we have been exploring the roles of biologically related grandparents and grandchildren. We should use this template as a role model for establishing a new and powerful social identity—and for putting it into action. Grandparents should become a vital part of the burgeoning intergenerational movement in America, one which has the potential to make a tremendous impact but which needs your input and support.

In retrospect, we can say that the movement's humble beginning happened more than thirty years ago, in 1963, when the National Foster Grandparent Program was established. The stated purpose of the program was to match lower-income elders with disabled children. The elders received a small stipend to work with the children on a one-to-one basis. The program has since expanded to include elders of all income levels and children with a wide variety of special needs.

Also in 1963, the Adopt-A-Grandparent Program was established in Florida. It involved weekly class visits by young children to a local nursing home. Other programs followed. In 1967, the Serve and Enrich Retirement by Volunteer Experience (SERVE) program was begun. Starting with a small group of elders working with retarded youngsters, SERVE became the precursor of the Retired Senior Volunteer Program (RSVP). The latter, founded in 1969, was authorized as a national program under the Older Americans Act of 1965. Then, in 1969, the National Center for Service Learning was established as the National Student Volunteer Program. In this program, students provided services to the elderly in their communities. It is now called Student Community Service. These programs are still active in communities all over the country. Then, as the new decade dawned, older people themselves joined together to support intergenerational activities. In 1970 the Gray Panthers was created as an advocacy group to combat ageism. In 1975, an agreement was reached to involve the elderly in the nation's schools, with the result that in 1975 Louis Harris and Associates reported that more than forty thousand elders were volunteering in schools. Also, in 1976 the nation's first aging curriculum was introduced in the California public schools. Then, in 1976, Teaching-Learning Communities was started in Michigan. This program brings elders and children together in the public schools. Government agencies also began to see the value of intergenerational programs. In 1977, the State of Florida created a school network using community elders.

From this point on, progress accelerated. Of particular note was the establishment of Generations Together at the University of Pittsburgh, the first university program to devote itself to intergenerational issues. Then, in 1979, intergenerational child-care centers were started by the Elvirita Lewis Foundation in California. To date, intergenerational programming and interchange has spread beyond schools and universities into a diversity of arenas such as religious, community, and government institutions. In fact, more than a hundred organizations have joined forces to start Generations United, a Washington-based organization dedicated to "promoting cross-generational understanding and cooperative action." According to Generations United director Tess Scannell,

"The formation of Generations United in 1986 was the culmination of social, political, and programmatic factors that had been brewing for more than twenty years. Socially, America, over the course of several decades, has become segregated by age; elderly people often live in age-segregated housing; children attend age-segregated schools; adults work in environments almost exclusive of children under sixteen. Isolation among generations is increased by the mobility of nuclear families and divorce. As a result there is a perception that the interests of the generations are at odds. Some fear this disparity of interest could lead to 'intergenerational wars.' "

This perception is correct. In the future, as the baby-boom generation ages, the relatively small "baby-bust" generation will be called upon in midlife to support increasing numbers of elders. Yet why should younger people who have not been intimately involved with their elders all along suddenly want to take care of them? The opposite is true too, however. My own grandparent studies have clearly demonstrated that young people who have had beloved grandparents or other elders in their lives are loving and sympathetic toward the older generations.

Thus the mission of the intergenerational movement is to coalesce the generations so that there will be a natural give-and-take among young and old. By definition, intergenerational programs refer to activities, programs, and events that form relationships and increase cooperation and mutual efforts between the generations. All of these intergenerational activities represent an extension into the community and society of the good aspects of grandparent/grandchild relationships. The benefits of intergenerational involvement to both generations duplicate much of the positive effects that happen between grandparents and grandchildren, in that elders involved in intergenerational relationships in the community carry out one or another role of grandparents: mentor, nurturer, historian, and all the rest.

Intergenerational activity is sorely needed, and you should get involved. I can guarantee that there is a program that is right for you. Some provide simple companionship and love, others offer tutoring, and still others offer sanctuary. There are intergenerational choruses, oral history projects, and visual art projects. The various programs take place in schools, places of worship, community centers, and even private homes. Check your local paper and supermarket bulletin boards and ask your clergy to direct you. You will find an activity that engages your skills, experience, and interests, and the rewards of involvement will be manifold.

However, even as the intergenerational movement shows encouraging growth that bodes well for the future of the vital connection in this society, there are still individual families in which grandparents and grandchildren are separated by the actions of angry members of the middle generation. This situation is nothing short of a tragedy. Over the years, I have worked long and hard to help people overcome this terrible problem. I have tried to change laws which allow parents to keep grandparents from being involved with their grandchildren, and I have worked with many people as they struggle to retain their grandparenthood. The following chapter spells out in detail what you can do if you ever find yourself in danger of losing your vital connection with your cherished grandchildren.

Whose Grandchild Is This, Anyway?

With the national divorce rate at an all-time high and with remarriage creating new family constellations at an alarming rate, grandparents today often find themselves lost in the process. Even when your children and children-in-law form fairly cordial post-divorce relationships, there is inevitable tension and confusion about custody and visitation in the immediate, let alone the extended, family. A seemingly simple issue such as trying to agree on where a child spends Christmas can become a battle royal. And of course when the divorce is not so cordial, grandparents are sometimes kept away from their grandchildren alto-

gether by new in-laws who have the mistaken idea that
"starting fresh" is good for the children.

The most tragic scenario of all, however, is one in
which a so-called intact family—the legal term for a married couple whose children reside with them—escalates
a family feud to the point that the middle generation
forbids the grandparents from contacting the grandchildren. In these cases, the law holds that the elders have
no right to visitation. In other words, grandparents
whose children are divorced stand at least a fighting
chance of regaining their vital connection, but grandparents whose children are married have no legal recourse
when the middle generation banishes them from the fold.
Here is the wording in a judge's decision from one such
case in Pennsylvania: "Appellants in the instant appeal
would have the court direct parents, both of whom have
chosen not to have their children visit the grandparents,
to permit such visitation. Nothing in the case or statutory
law legitimizes such an intrusion by the courts into family life."

To my amazement, court cases like this one continue
to demonstrate that the legal system upholds the short-
sighted principle of the "intact" family as one which, in
the words of a report by the Select Committee on Aging
of the House of Representatives, "is ordinarily defined
so as not to include grandparents." In my view, this basic
premise flies in the face of the most basic biological, psychological, social, and spiritual imperatives. The notion
that a family consists of only two generations, and that
parents have total say over the lives of their children,
seems to me nothing short of preposterous. I believe that

a family which excludes grandparents—if they are available, of course, and if gross pathology isn't present—is not intact at all. A family with living but exiled grandparents is a dismembered family. How did it happen that the law has come to see the grandparents as intruders instead of family members? The intact concept is destructive, not constructive. It promotes emotional wounds instead of emotional healing. And over and over again I have seen that the result is that everyone, including the middle generation, suffers profoundly.

Furthermore, the intactness of a marriage is absolutely no indicator of the health of the marriage, or of its noxiousness to a child. Fortunately, most parents are caring and loving to their children. But those who are abusive and destructive in first or multiple marriages can hide behind the intact doctrine. Everybody knows that all kinds of mayhem occurs behind closed doors in intact families, from garden-variety conflicts to life-threatening situations. When grandparents are rendered powerless to step in with advice and help, tragedies can occur, both emotional and physical.

Also, many years of dealing with family issues have indicated to me that intergenerational family problems are often temporary. People simply grow out of them. But when the law has literally been laid down early on, there is no chance later for a change of heart. I recall one young mother, Allie, who was angry at her mother because she disapproved of the man Allie married. Allie vindictively banished her mother from her life and the lives of her children. "Mom messed me up," she said at the time. "I'm not going to give her a chance to mess up my kids." Fortunately, however, no legal action was ever taken in this case, and with time and counseling, Allie softened her position. As she learned firsthand about the ins and outs of raising children, and found out what it was like to have a child talk back to her, she began to have more sympathy for her mother's point of view. Finally, she was able to forgive her mother and welcome her back into the life of the family. Such is the way of the world. People mature, problems have a way of working out, and life goes on. But cut-and-dried legal doctrine has the effect of making permanent problems out of temporary conflicts.

That is why it is vital that you work at building a strong relationship with your children and children-in-law, starting long before the wedding and continuing throughout the years. When you do that, you're in the best position to handle conflicts when they arise, and to avoid the courtroom alternative altogether. However, if in spite of your best efforts and intentions, you find that you can't settle your differences by yourselves, you may well benefit from some professional help in the form of a mediator. Certainly, you should try the age-old healing process of mediation before you so much as think about taking your case to court, even if your children are divorced and there is a chance that the law might rule in your favor regarding visitation. And as we have seen, if you are feuding with children in an intact marriage, going to court wouldn't do any good anyway. But with the assistance of a mediator, everyone concerned has the best chance of realizing that the children should not become the innocent victims of adult problems. Remember, the legal process is by definition adversarial, with the goal being to determine a "winner" and a "loser" in family conflicts. The purpose of mediation, on the contrary, is to help the family remain connected even as the various members work through problems. In the words of Leonard Loeb, former president of the American Academy of Matrimonial Lawyers and the Family Law Section representative to the American Bar Association's House of Delegates, "The last place grandparents should go is to court. They should try to use every other means of dispute resolution available. Going to the court really doesn't produce the maximum result. At best, it produces the minimum result."

In fact, when grandparents go to court, they are walking into a lion's den. While there is a chance that the court might actually grant visitation if the parents are divorced, the fact is that grandparents and grandchildren can also lose one another in the courtroom. Nowhere will all the negative aspects of familial conflicts seem more intractable, and nowhere will family members be divided against one another more sharply, than in the courtroom.

Not only that, but because of the way in which the judicial system works, whether or not a grandparent is ultimately granted visitation is often a toss-up. A court of law concerns itself with the administration of "justice" by considering "facts" derived from what it considers to be objective reality. To discern these facts, the court uses a prescribed procedural manner, considering evidence and enunciating an allegedly objective judgment concerning what, and who, is "right" or "wrong" in the case at hand. Then it resolves the issue, usually according to legal precedent.

While this method works fairly well in cases concerning burglary or tax evasion, it really is not applicable to family problems. Where family conflicts are concerned, it is almost always impossible to determine objective

truths and facts. Most "facts" in the family context are really matters of personal opinion, and personal opinions are based on people's own perceptions of themselves, their perceptions of one another, and their reactions to these perceptions—all of which, to complicate things even further, are themselves dependent on the personalities of the people involved. Every individual is a separate universe, with a complete set of personal idiosyncrasies. When these universes collide, anything can happen.

A Friendly Intervention

How much better, then, to avoid that collision. The way to do so is to try mediation. Sometimes called a "friendly intervention," this is a method of resolving conflicts between people by keeping the lines of communication open. The purpose of mediation, which is the basis of family therapy, is to heal family wounds and renew family bonds through a process of negotiation which considers the attitudes and experience of all family members.

In a mediation session, the two or more opposing parties are brought together in a neutral setting to discuss their grievances in a nonconfrontational and noncombative way. Actually, mediation is something people have always done, even before it was formally named. When a mother helps settle a sibling squabble or a friend acts as a sympathetic go-between for a couple in conflict, mediation occurs naturally. It is a flexible process and can be used in a variety of situations. You have probably heard the word *mediation* applied as a method of legal dispute resolution (between labor and management groups in business, for example), in the law (as it relates

to plea bargaining), and so on. But it is an especially useful and natural process for negotiating family conflicts, too. The mediator hears all sides of a story and tries to help the quarreling parties arrive at a mutually satisfactory resolution. Any parent who has tried to settle a fight between children has already been a mediator, and knows exactly what the process is all about.

In some instances of conflict between grandparents and parents, family members or friends can act as go-betweens, or amateur mediators. However, family members and friends are likely to lose their objectivity and cause more problems than they solve. This is why a professional is a much better choice. Professional mediators, because of their training, detachment, and authoritative position, are more objective in family disputes than even the best-intentioned amateur mediators. There are mediative therapists in private practice and also not-for-profit family service agencies with sliding fee scales to suit your financial situation. Check your local Yellow Pages or ask your clergy for a referral.

I have found that the mediative approach to solving grandparent visitation conflicts, no matter what the stage of family disruption, is the most useful, least harmful, and least expensive. And most important, mediation makes it much more likely that grandparents really will continue to have contact with their grandchildren. After all, even if grandparents win visitation rights through the courts, the truth is that the grandparents' access to the children most often remains dependent on the cooperation of the children's caretaker. Without that cooperation, winning visitation is only a Pyrrhic victory. True, in one celebrated New York case, a mother was eventually held in contempt of court after she repeatedly

failed to abide by a judge's decision to facilitate visitation between her children and their grandparents. The judge ruled that "divorced parents have no right to interfere with court-ordered visits between children and their grandparents." But there is never a guarantee that the court will come to the rescue in these cases. You are much better off trying to negotiate a mutually satisfactory arrangement through a mediator. In other words, work toward healing differences—a happier, healthier, and cheaper alternative.

What's Good About Mediation Therapy: A Success Story

One of the first families I worked with as a mediator-therapist came to the initial session with a list of complaints and conflicts, and an equally long list of players in the conflicts.

Serena, a mother of four, had a good relationship with Jack and Beth Rinaldi, her parents-in-law. After ten years of marriage, Serena's husband was killed in an industrial accident. Two years later, Serena remarried, but she maintained her relationship with the Rinaldis. Serena's new husband, Carl Miller, didn't like the Rinaldis. When Carl adopted Serena's children, he wanted to discontinue contact between the Rinaldis and their grandchildren. He felt that they not only reminisced too often about the children's deceased father, but that they continually compared him to Carl, putting Carl in a bad light. Carl was sure that the longer he allowed the kids to see the Rinaldis, the harder it would be for them to accept him as their new dad.

The Rinaldis didn't understand why Carl didn't want

them to talk about their son to the kids, so they continued to do so. Serena just wanted peace, but that didn't happen. Things got worse. The Rinaldis criticized Carl, and he responded by being rude to them. Eventually, Carl put a stop to the Rinaldis' visits altogether. Carl told Serena and the children not to talk to the Rinaldis. He hung up when they called, sent back their gifts, and eventually had a lawyer write them a letter saying that Carl would sue them for harassment if they continued to pursue seeing their grandchildren.

The Rinaldis, panic-stricken, finally went to see a lawyer, but he told them there was not much to be done because at the time, there were no laws in their state providing them with the opportunity to petition for visitation with their grandchildren. On their way home from the attorney's office, the Rinaldis stopped off at their church to ask the advice of Father Phillips. Father Phillips was friendly with and had the respect of everyone involved in the conflict. Even the "newcomer," Carl, was actively involved in Father Phillips's church. Father Phillips recommended that all of the people involved spend several therapy sessions with me in an attempt to iron out their interpersonal problems and negotiate their differences.

Serena readily agreed to this, because she knew the Rinaldis were important to her children. Carl agreed because he wanted Serena to be happy. The Rinaldis were relieved that there was some hope they would be able to be grandparents to their grandchildren again, and the children, needless to say, were very happy that someone was going to keep the adults from squabbling.

In the first session, I pointed out that they all had something very important in common: their love for the children. From that positive starting point we worked for many sessions to a resolution of the problems. Eventually, as a result of therapy, Carl was able to identify and deal with the reason for his dislike of the Rinaldis. It actually had little to do with the Rinaldis themselves, and more to do with his own feelings about Serena's children not being his own. It also came out that Carl had not had a terrific relationship with his own authoritative parents.

For their part, the Rinaldis learned to respect Carl as an individual and not compare him to their own son, and to support and befriend Carl. It took over a year to get to this point. In the meantime, I recommended that Carl allow the Rinaldis more and more time with their grandchildren. At first, visits were confined to the Millers' home, and they were supervised by Serena. Then, as the Rinaldis became more supportive of Carl, he allowed them to spend time alone with their grandchildren. At the end of our year together, the children were spending entire weekends at the Rinaldis' home.

One of the most worthwhile and surprising results of this whole affair was the children's increased regard for Carl. As Carl changed his attitudes toward the Rinaldis, the children were gradually taken out of the difficult position of having to choose between people they loved. Ten-year-old Craig Miller described his feelings: "I hated it whenever Mom and Carl talked about my grandparents, and I hated Carl. Before, I couldn't stand being around them when they were all together and watching them act so angry and weird. Now Carl's cool. He drives me to my grandparents' house and he talks to them really nice. I don't know what everyone was fighting about, but now they're happy and I know they all love me. I love everybody, too."

This case demonstrates how well the mediative-therapeutic process can work. As soon as a mediator steps in, the destructive tailspin that characterizes so many family conflicts is halted, preventing further destruction. Involving a mediator shows everyone that there is a chance for a positive solution to their troubles. Hopelessness is dispelled. Healing begins almost immediately.

Weighing the Courtroom Alternative

Through principled negotiation and gentle mediation with willing participants, then, most family conflicts can be brought to satisfactory resolutions. Sometimes, however, one of the parties refuses to engage in the healing process. In such a case, particularly when grandchildren are given up to foster care or transported far away by their caretakers, grandparents may consider invoking the law. Do keep in mind, though, that while courts implicitly recognize the importance of a parent's relationship with a child, in the language of the laws in most states, until very recently, there was no recognition of the nature of the unique relationship between a grandparent and a child, or the child's need for a grandparent.

Still, the advent of grandparent visitation legislation which I, along with scores of other dedicated people, helped to implement represents an important first step in society's recognition of the importance of the grandparenting role. As a result of that legislation, grandparents can now petition the courts for visitation in every state in the case of parental death, separation, and divorce and, in some states, stepparent adoption, although not when a parental marriage is still intact. Just the existence of these laws is important, because those caretakers who would sever the bond between grandchildren and their grandparents often think twice about doing this, knowing that they might be taken to court as a result.

Sadly, however, even if a grandparent does obtain a court order for visitation, all a parent has to do to thwart visitation is to move out of state. The grandparent must then commit the time and energy, and often a staggering sum of money, to restart the litigation process. And most people just can't afford that. Here is a case in point. After several years of marriage, Tom and Julie Killian got divorced. Julie retained custody of their two young children, Sheila and Erin. However, Julie had a very amicable relationship with Tom's mother Wilma, and Wilma was very close to the two children, so Julie allowed Wilma to see the children anytime that she liked. Julie also frequently relied on Wilma to take the children overnight or for a weekend when she needed a break. This arrangement went on quite nicely for a couple of years after the divorce.

Gradually, however, Wilma noticed that Julie was becoming somewhat lethargic and irritable. Wilma also learned that Julie was allowing different men to sleep at her house, which was an uncharacteristic departure from Julie's strict moral code. Also, the children had begun complaining that their mother wasn't getting up in the morning to see them off to school. Wilma expressed her concern to Julie. The following week she received a letter from Julie which said: "Dear Mrs. Killian: I have decided it isn't good for us to be a family anymore. I wish you happiness in the future. Ours looks very bright. All plans made for your visits are hereby canceled. You would be wise not to come here anymore. Please don't call or I will hang up."

Concerned about Sheila and Erin, Wilma tried to contact Julie without success. After appealing to a series of people and agencies, Wilma consulted a lawyer about the possibility of pursuing legal action to resolve her situation, but the cost of having a lawyer represent her in court was too high. Wilma decided to plead her own case. Surprisingly, Wilma won the right to visit with her grandchildren once a month for eight hours. The judge presiding over the case allowed this in spite of Julie's animosity for Wilma.

But that is far from the end of the story. Although Wilma was awarded visitation by the court, Julie did her best to hinder the visits. She repeatedly changed visitation dates and canceled them at the last minute. When a date was finally agreed upon, Wilma would arrive at Julie's home to pick up the children and find no one there.

Wilma, angry and upset, asked the court to intercede. The judge ordered Julie to comply with the visitation arrangements, and asked the local sheriff to enforce the order. For a while after the court's intervention, Wilma was able to visit Sheila and Erin regularly.

Then, one day, Wilma arrived to pick up her grandchildren and found a real estate agent showing the empty house to prospective buyers. Wilma called Julie's mother—who was as upset about her daughter's behavior as Wilma was—only to learn that Julie had moved to another state. Wilma wanted nothing more than to set out after Julie and her grandchildren, but she had neither the money, the emotional resources, nor the support of the law. So Wilma lost her grandchildren—and Sheila and Erin lost their grandmother.

Ten years later, at the age of nineteen, Sheila showed up at Wilma's house. Sheila told Wilma that she had been dragged around from state to state by her substance-abusing mother and the men she attracted. She told of her sexual molestation by a stepfather for two years. She described how she had been taken away from her mother by the "social service" and put into a foster home. And she told Wilma that at no time did her foster parents or anyone at any social agency heed her requests to contact her grandmother. Finally, Sheila tracked Wilma down herself.

Unfortunately, this is not an unusual story, but the fact is that we are just beginning to learn about what happens to children who are deprived of their grandparents. Many of the children I interviewed when I began my research more than twenty years ago are coming back to me as adults to tell me what they experienced when they lost their grandparents. Freed from parental restraints, they are beginning to search for their grandparents.

Also, a number of the parents involved in the cases I studied have contacted me to tell me that they regretted having separated their children from their parents or parents-in-law. Several parents that I know made an effort to repair the damage by reuniting grandparents and grandchildren. It has taken a long time, but many tragic stories have turned out happily in the end.

Among the most heartwarming stories are those involving some of the pioneers in the fight for grandparent visitation laws, those who sacrificed huge amounts of time and energy to make it a little easier for other grandparents to maintain their grandparenthood. As a reward for their extraordinary efforts, many of these grandparents have been reunited with their grandchildren. These grandchildren have told me how painful it was for them when their grandparents were taken away, and they have expressed concern for the millions of children who are going through what they experienced.

They have also told me how their suffering could have been avoided. Sheila, for example, told me her agony could have been prevented if her grandmother's visitation privileges hadn't been lost as a result of her mother's move to another state. "I had continually asked my mother if I could call my grandmother," she said, "but my mother told everyone that my grandmother was a terrible person, and all the other adults believed her, so no one would ever let me call. Eventually, I was afraid to call myself, because everyone told me my grandmother was bad.

"At one point, my mother told me my grandmother was dead. Later, when my mother was in rehab, she admitted that she had lied to me. Mom told me she moved to keep my grandmother from me because my grandmother would've blown the whistle on her. She explained that by moving, she made it so that my grandmother couldn't visit with us because the laws were different in different states. My mom said she was sorry she did that to me, but she couldn't help it because she was sick. When I found all that out, I decided to search for my grandmother."

A uniform state grandparent visitation law could prevent some of this pain. Sheila said that a great deal of her misery could have been prevented if her mother had not been able to avoid Wilma's visits simply by moving from state to state. By providing for the enforcement in one state of a visitation order issued in another state, a uniform state grandparent visitation law would prevent just such a situation. As it now stands, however, because of state-to-state variations in grandparent visitation laws, the legal wranglings necessary to enforce a visitation order in another state are too complex, too exhausting, and too expensive for most grandparents to pursue, especially if the grandparents have just gone through a drawn-out court battle in their home state. Sadly, even though Congress made an attempt a decade ago to put a uniform visitation law into practice, to date this hasn't happened.

One of the main reasons for the defeat was arguments put forth that by their nature, family problems do not lend themselves to laws but should be dealt with directly by the family, and that state-level intervention is less intrusive than federal intervention. While these arguments do have some merit, they still don't address the issue at hand. The fact remains that state-level legislation leaves a legal chasm that people like Sheila and Wilma fall through every day. Such a position offers no recourse for the emotional suffering of grandparent and grandchild when a caretaker flees a state in which grandparents have visitation rights. The lack of uniform legislation also gives caretakers a potent weapon to use against grandparents: if the grandparents intend to sue, the parents just threaten to move.

Other opponents to grandparent visitation legislation argue that it's better to allow caretakers to separate grandchildren from their grandparents than to run the risk of having the caretakers and grandparents use the children as pawns in their battles and involve them in a conflict of loyalty. This is where I feel that the experts who say that family issues should never be exposed to the legal process are neglecting an important point: how the law can be used in a *positive* manner to ensure the integrity of grandparent/grandchild relationships and to initiate a healing process. I believe that when parties are at an impasse, we should use the power of the courts to coerce people to deal with their problems, preferably with the help of a mediator, while grandparents and grandchildren keep at least some form of contact. At the very least, this constitutes damage control. Concepts like the "intact family" doctrine and limiting grandparent visitation to one state at a time do not reflect the realities of family life and human relationships. They represent more of a throw-in-the-towel policy. The excuse given is that the legal system doesn't want to tarnish its hands with family issues—but it does so anyway.

We have enough knowledge and available experts to deal with these issues in helpful and realistic ways and to prevent unnecessary family carnage. The solution is mediation, and the principle is "Work out your problems and don't dismember your family." If we can establish this way of doing things, all family members will benefit and the young will be protected from the folly of their forebears. The middle generation in particular needs to be protected from its own impulsive decisions and actions. Mandated mediation laws say, in effect: "Your family is going to stay together whether you like it or not. Learn to live together, grow up and make the best of it. That's the finest example to show your children. You may be in the same boat one day."

This would send a positive message to everyone. The children would hear: "You can't get rid of relatives you disagree with. Work it out." The middle generation would hear: "You'll be in your parents' shoes one day. Try to see this through their eyes now. Talk things through. Forgive. Find a new balance to the relationship." And the grandparents would hear: "Learn to know your adult children. What is their world like? How are they struggling? How can you help, and be the parent and grandparent the family needs?"

Healing and reunion are what we should aim for, instead of divisive "us and them" laws and policies. But that is a moot point, because despite all of the hard work and compelling testimony, the National Conference of Commissioners on Uniform State Laws did not recommend a uniform state law governing grandparental visitation in their 1984 deliberations. They felt that this was an issue of state jurisdiction, not federal. As of this writing, the members of the conference have not reconsidered the issue. However, while there is no distinct and separate uniform grandparent visitation law, some legal scholars feel that the language of the Uniform Marriage and Divorce Act already provides grandparents with the right to visitation. Certain parts of the act say that serving the best interest of a child allows judges to "permit intervention of other interested parties," and that the judge can order visitation with parents, siblings, "and any other person who may significantly affect the child's best interest."

Some people see these provisions as a window of opportunity for grandparents, but they are vague, are erratically applied, and require fast action. In many states, grandparental visitation arrangements must be submitted before a final divorce agreement is written. This loophole is obviously no substitute for real grandparent visitation legislation. The fight to pass a uniform grandparent visitation law was bitter and difficult, and in the end, it did not achieve its primary goal.

When the Courtroom
Is the Only Answer

There are, and always will be, cases in which mediation fails and asking the court for help becomes the only alternative. If you are involved in a family dispute with divorced, widowed, or remarried children and you are prevented from seeing your grandchildren in spite of having tried all other feasible avenues, then it is time for you to go to court. Although nothing is guaranteed once litigants enter the courtroom, there are certain steps that you should and must take in order to put yourself in the best possible position for achieving your goals.

Once a family dispute is brought into the legal arena, it is often difficult to keep things in perspective. The most important thing to remember, however, is that everything you do should be done with the ultimate well-being of your grandchild in mind. This is the cardinal rule to which all of the attorneys, therapists, counselors, and judges who may eventually become involved will apply, and it should be your motivation also. It is important for you to establish in your own mind, as well as the minds of others, that the continuation of your relationship with your grandchild is absolutely necessary to your grandchild.

This is important not only from a moral standpoint, but from a strategic one as well. Leonard Loeb, mentioned early in this chapter, says, "A grandparent should go into court on the premise that visitation is the grand-child's right, not the grandparents'. That is a much easier position to sustain, since the court has no obligation to look after the well-being of the grandparent, but it does have to look after the best interests of the child."

Unfortunately, it can be difficult to demonstrate that maintaining a relationship with the grandparents is in the best interest of the child. Traditionally, the criteria used by the court have focused on the convenience and wishes of the middle generation, while ignoring altogether the deep genetic and spiritual bond between the elder generation and the children. This is particularly sad in light of the fact that experience and research have shown that the relationship between grandparents and grandchildren is separate and distinct from that of parents and children. It has a character and purpose all its own, and it has nothing to do with whether or not the parents and grandparents are at odds. To deny children access to their heritage and to prevent them from carrying that legacy into the future is a grave error which inflicts profound psychological wounds on all concerned. And yet the law in most cases continues to use only the most superficial definitions of "the best interest of the child" and to rule that grandparent visitation should not be granted if it would be disruptive to the middle generation. This, in my view, constitutes abuse of the children, not their best interest.

However, given the realities of the current legal system, the best you can do is to state your case as truthfully and sensitively as possible, emphasizing that your relationship with the children is good for them in myriad important ways—and then pray for a judge who is wise enough to think with his heart.

FINDING AN ATTORNEY

The first step you need to take is to find an attorney. Even if you already have a family attorney, that person is not necessarily the best one for the job. Richard S. Victor, a lawyer in private practice with extensive experience in grandparent visitation cases, explains: "As with medicine, law today has become extremely specialized. A grandparent looking to find representation should seek an attorney who specializes in family law with an emphasis on custody and visitation matters. A grandparent who is to become a potential client should seek out names of attorneys who have handled divorce matters where custody of the children involved was an issue." An excellent way to do this is to contact one of the grandparent support groups listed in the appendix of this book. Members can give you personal referrals. However, if you find that costs are too prohibitive, limited legal aid may be available to you. Your local legal aid service or society can tell you how to go about securing legal aid, but the process involved is usually a very lengthy one.

COURTROOM PREPARATION

After you have settled on an attorney, it is really up to the attorney to start the procedural ball rolling. You should remain involved in every step of the process, however. Indeed, to secure the necessary information, a lawyer may request several more meetings, and you should not be afraid to ask for frequent updates and appraisals as to the "winnability" of the case.

You should also ask the attorney to keep you apprised of any alternatives as they come up. Even after you've gotten this far, alternatives to direct litigation may still exist. If the visitation issue arises from a case involving divorce, the divorce agreement may contain elements that could allow for grandparental visitation. And if a final divorce agreement has not been entered, it is possible that grandparental visitation could still be written into it. In that case, it would be up to your attorney to contact the other attorneys involved in the case to try to work out an agreement.

Also, attorneys themselves may make attempts to get you and the other feuding parties into mediation one last time before going to court. As Mr. Loeb says: "At the very least, an attorney considering filing a grandparent visitation suit should discuss the alternative of mediation as a means of resolving the dispute before the actual litigation process begins." And in a recent document, the American Bar Association recommends that "attorneys, court personnel and other professionals should be encouraged to refer persons involved in grandparent visitation disputes to appropriate mediation services. If possible such referrals should be made prior to the filing of any court action."

If all parties agree to one last attempt at mediation, the attorneys themselves may serve as mediators, or they may refer you to other mediators or even collaborate with another mediator. In a divorce case, for example, a mediator may be brought in to work out logistics of grandparental visitation and then collaborate with the attorney to have these written into the divorce agreement.

In some cases, however, participation in the mediative process is not a matter of choice. Certain states have passed grandparent visitation laws that allow the judge to order an embattled family to accept mediation. Laws such as these make a major contribution to the welfare of the family by deemphasizing the adversarial process involved in courtroom proceedings, recognizing the value of mediation, and making it a policy to "sentence" even the most contentious people to mediation not only to work out visitation schedules, but to attempt to ameliorate all of their problems. People who refused would literally be in contempt of court.

I am the first to admit that sometimes those problems are caused more by the grandparents than by the middle generation. After all, many grandparents have serious problems of their own, such as alcohol abuse, emotional instability, or criminal behavior, and their contact with their grandchildren *should* be supervised. Even so, it almost always is in the best interest of the child that the grandparent/grandchild relationship be maintained. For example, one young grandfather, fifty-two-year-old investment banker Al Jones, is serving a prison term for stock fraud and embezzlement. Before he was sentenced, Al was very close to his six-year-old granddaughter, Irma. Al's son, embarrassed by his father's notoriety, refused to let Irma visit Al in jail. Al appealed to his lawyer, who mediated an arrangement whereby Irma is allowed to visit Al in jail, a minimum-security facility, twice a year. This arrangement has greatly cheered and inspired Al and he has pledged that he will be out of jail on parole in time to go to Irma's wedding and to see his great-grandchildren born. As for Irma, she understands that Grandpa did a bad thing, but that he's going to be good now. She also says she loves him very much and that she always will.

When people attempt to separate grandparents and grandchildren permanently, they inflict wounds at the most profound levels of the psyche and the spirit, and everyone, including parents or caretakers, suffers. The courts have a duty to protect parents from their own impulses by mandating healing via mediation. In so doing, the courts can avert the serious, often irreversible psychological damage that can result from depriving grandparents and grandchildren of one another, as well as the lingering guilt which plagues the middle generation when they rend the other generations asunder. Mandated mediation serves this purpose well, because compliance with the agreements reached is closely monitored and reported back to the court by the mediator. Any infractions can be swiftly handled. Or to put it more positively, this way of working things out makes the parties face their problems and deal with them.

Here is a particularly heartwarming case in which mandated mediation worked wonders. A couple named Leon and Ellen Wade went to court to try to arrange for visitation with their grandchild, and their ex-son-in-law's attorney tried to draw out the case as long as possible. He knew that the Wades' funds were limited and that they could not afford legal services for long. The judge who was hearing the case saw the inequity in the situation. He appointed a local family therapist to interview the family members and make recommendations to the court.

The therapist was able to bring about a negotiated visitation agreement that spared all family members the pain and suffering that could easily have resulted from a continuation of the legal battle. He did this by probing deeper into the complexities and ramifications of the situation than could ever be done in an adversarial courtroom setting. For example, he interviewed a diversity of friends and relatives of those involved to determine the degree of closeness between the children and the Wades. This sort of information would have been far too time-consuming and costly to elicit in court, yet it was crucial in determining an equitable solution to the problem.

Of course, not even mandated mediation succeeds in all cases. If litigation becomes inevitable, thinking in terms of how the court perceives the case becomes of paramount importance.

What to Expect in the Courtroom

On the surface, the courtroom procedure may seem to be very logical. Two opposing attorneys will try to show the judge that their own clients are "in the right." To do this, each will submit evidence, call witnesses, and cross-examine witnesses called by the opposing attorney. The trouble is that once the proceedings get under way, the intense emotions and passions of those involved can easily cloud issues, distort facts, and frustrate intentions. Again, it is important to focus on one thing throughout the courtroom battle: the best interest of the child. That is what the attorneys will be trying to establish, and what the judge will ultimately be looking for.

Keeping a level head in the heat of battle not only keeps things running smoothly, it also furthers the grandparents' cause. "It is not uncommon for bitter, vindictive feelings to surface during the proceedings. Keeping them away from the judge may be difficult, but doing so is imperative. A judge in Cook County, Illinois, ruled, after these feelings were brought out in testimony, that it was not in the best interest of the children to be exposed to such feelings. Beware of revealing too much hostility, and do not let your opponents use this against you."

Also, try to come across as rational, practical people by making it clear to the court that your goal in pursuing litigation is to achieve visitation only. Oftentimes parents will try to label the fight as a custody battle, but you stand a better chance of winning if you limit your aims to visitation only.

With his years of courtroom experience, Mr. Victor concurs: "The most important aspect of a grandparent's visitation case is to show the court that the grandparent's request is to provide the minor child involved with the ability to continue and maintain the close and continuing relationship which previously existed. The best strategy is to show that the grandparent is not fighting this action for himself or herself, but rather is bringing this action for and in the benefit of the minor child."

Judges in particular are guided by the best-interest-of-the-child principle. The Honorable Ernest Rotenberg is first judge of the Bristol County Probate and Family Court Department of Massachusetts and an adjunct professor at Suffolk University Law School. He has presided over a number of grandparent visitation cases. In the American Bar Association's *Grandparent Visitation Disputes Manual,* he outlines what it is that he looks for to determine if a visitation order is warranted:

1. It must be demonstrated that it is important in general and in the particular circumstances of this case that visitation be established with the paternal or maternal grandparents (or both).

2. A thoughtful, well-conceived plan for visitation with the grandparents should be prepared and submitted to the court.

3. The petitioner should demonstrate that there has

been a visitation history between the child and the particular grandparents in the past that should be perpetuated.

4. If there has been a visitation history, the petitioner should prove that the visits were satisfactory and beneficial to the child.

How the Best Interest Is Demonstrated

The attorneys involved in your case will most often use the testimony of both you and others intimately familiar with your case and that of "expert" outsiders to try to establish the best interest of your grandchildren. Lawyers with extensive experience in family issues will usually have access to one or more psychologists who can interview the children and make recommendations to the court. If you are important to the children, this interview should bring that out. In addition, your attorney may call other therapists and counselors to testify on the importance of grandparents in general. The judge may also interview the children in camera, that is, in his or her chambers in a relaxed setting, in order to determine the true wishes of the children.

An attorney will also call other witnesses, such as friends, baby-sitters, and relatives, to help establish the nature of the relationship between you and your grandchildren. You should be prepared to provide the attorney with the names of witnesses who can testify about the stability of your relationship with the children (occurrence witnesses) and about your own emotional stability (character witnesses).

Eventually, the attorney will probably call you to the witness stand. To prepare for that potentially nerve-racking experience, Victor recommends, "When a grandparent takes the witness stand in a hearing, the attorney representing the grandparent should have reviewed with the grandparent the state law language which defines 'best interest of the child.' The statutory language is very important for the grandparent to know prior to becoming a witness at any hearing."

Usually, your attorney will review with you the questions he or she will ask before calling you to the witness stand. You will no doubt be asked to compile information regarding the home lives, habits, activities, jobs, and religions of not only yourself, but everyone involved in the conflict. It is also helpful to have at hand any information about the parents' previous marriages, other familial relationships, and your relationship with your spouse.

But the most important information you need to have is hard-core evidence that the relationship between you and your grandchildren is real, thriving, and stable. The best plan is to prepare a written summary of your relationship. The important elements of such a summary should include:

• Whether you were present when the children were born.

• How often you and your grandchildren saw each other from the time they were born.

• What activities you shared, such as reading to them, taking them on special excursions, or having them over to your home.

• Whether you acted as a baby-sitter.

• Intimate details which you know about your grand-children's lives, such as the names of friends, pets, favorite colors, favorite games and stories, and favorite foods.

You should also try to have a clear idea of exactly why you are in the situation. Was visitation with your grand-children an issue in the rift between you and their care-takers? Are the caretakers using cessation of visitation as a weapon in a fight that has nothing to do with the grandchildren? Remember, the ultimate goal is for you to show in a visitation hearing that your relationship with your grandchildren is healthy, thriving, and above all necessary to the mental and emotional well-being of the children.

One reason that it is important for you to have all of this information clearly planted in your mind is that you may also face a potentially hostile cross-examination by the opposing attorney. You have no way of actually pre-paring for that experience, but Mr. Loeb says that your best tack is to "relax, be honest, and just explain the situation as you view it." Most questions will center around issues we have already covered, such as the ex-tent of the relationship between you and your grand-children, and the nature of your relationship with the parents and other family members.

THE GUARDIAN AD LITEM
In cases involving young children, it is not unusual for one or both parties involved to request that the court appoint a guardian ad litem (GAL) to look after the in-terests of the child. Sometimes the court will do this on its own. The GAL is an attorney who represents the

child's viewpoint, even if the child is in the care and custody of his or her parents. The GAL, in effect, speaks for
children who cannot, because of their age or situation,
speak for themselves. In most cases, the GAL has the
power to sue even the parents, if the GAL perceives that
their behavior is detrimental to the child. This is important, because, as Judge Rotenberg says, "A parent does
not have an immutable right to the association with children. Parental rights must yield to the best interest and
welfare of the children."

WHEN THE COURTROOM BATTLE IS DONE

After all the testimony has been rendered and the dust
has settled, the only thing left to do is wait for the judge
to render a decision. If the court decides to allow visitation, it is then necessary to agree on the specifics of the
visitation order. One of the most important things for
you to look for in a visitation order is flexibility. Does
the order allow for increased visitation with time? Does
it allow for a variety of locations, since it is best not to
hold early visitations in the home of the child?

If the court does not decide in favor of visitation, you
may want to file an appeal. Of course, this will mean
more expense, and probably more anguish. Your attorney can supply information as to how your state works
its appeals court system.

Even if the court does decide in your favor, there will
probably be numerous emotional wounds that will need
healing if the bond between you and the parents, and
even the bond between you and your grandchildren, is
ever to be truly healthy again. If it is at all possible—and
it often is once a courtroom battle is a thing of the past—
all the parties involved should try to get some kind

of professional counseling. Again, even the help of an amateur mediator would be beneficial. The most important thing after a combative, divisive courtroom battle has taken place is to get the family back on track toward emotional stability as soon as possible. Only then can your grandparent/grandchild bond, and all of your family bonds, become all that they should be. Remember, family problems don't have to be permanent. An essential part of our humanity is that we grow and change. With growth and change comes increased wisdom. With wisdom comes understanding. And with understanding comes an ever-increasing capacity for forgiveness. This happens not only on the part of the grandparents but on the part of the parents as they age as well.

This phenomenon, of course, is not limited to people who suffer through painful family rifts. All of us grow wiser and more tolerant with age and experience. We become the sages of society. And as this happens, we must not retire from the most important work of our lives—that of nurturing our families and our communities, and keeping the vital connection alive. If that sounds suspiciously like a battle cry—albeit for a peacekeeping cause—that's exactly what it is. This is why I have saved the final pages of this book for what I hope will serve as a clarion call to arms.

Afterword

WHAT IS A LONG LIFE FOR?

This is a book for all grandparents today, but it holds a particularly potent message for the newest of the nation's elders. Your generation has been changing the course of history ever since you were born. That is your destiny. Age will not diminish your power, but will instead enhance your importance. You are legion, and you have a job to do in your later years. That there are so many of you, and that you are living so much longer than any generation before you, means that you have a vital purpose, now more than ever. There are two uncharted emotional and social territories you still have to traverse—grandparenting and great-grandparenting. You need to be intrepid explorers in *these areas because no generation before you has had the opportunity to experience both the pressures and pleasures of these life stages in such great numbers and with such continuing health and vitality. Even now, statistics show that one in ten thousand Americans is one hundred years of age or older. We have every reason to believe that your generation will up that remarkable number by much more. This being so, you are the first to look forward as a group to living and growing long past the midlife years when people have to focus on mundane issues. Decades stretch ahead of you in which you can move into a more numinous domain.*

As you grow spiritually, you will retain unprecedented physical prowess and vitality and collectively debunk the myth that later life must be synonymous with debilitating loss of both physical and mental agility. Science is sweeping away old notions about the inevitability of decline in old age, and replacing them with exciting discoveries about how people who refuse to sit down in the proverbial rocking chair and "accept" the weakness of aging are staying far more fit than anyone had ever thought possible. Deepak Chopra, M.D., author of the best-selling *Ageless Body, Timeless Mind,* bases much of his own encouraging work on the groundbreaking studies done by Walter M. Boritz, M.D., of Stanford University. Boritz examined the phenomena of atrophy and entrophy, the withering of the body's tissues, and found that lack of use was the single most important cause for this occurrence. He dubbed the situation the "disuse syndrome," and went on to show that not only physical deterioration, but mental and emotional symptoms such as severe depression, result when human beings become inactive.

In the same vein, a government-sponsored study on human aging done at Tufts University has demonstrated that increased activity along with an improved diet can not only slow the aging process, but actually reverse its ill effects even if they are already under way. The principal researchers, William Evans and Brian Rosenberg, published the findings in their book *Biomarkers,* stating that there are ten essential functions which need not be ravaged by time:

1. Lean body (muscle) mass
2. Strength
3. Basal metabolic rate
4. Body fat
5. Aerobic capacity
6. Blood pressure
7. Blood-sugar tolerance
8. Cholesterol/HDL ratio
9. Bone density
10. Body temperature regulation

But what about the brain? Isn't it true that "the mind goes" as we age? Absolutely not. Unless a disease process such as Alzheimer's is present—a disorder which is thought to be inherited and which afflicts only a small percentage of the population—people who stay vital and active can remain mentally vigorous as long as they live.

Witness the accomplishments of such legends as Pablo
Picasso and Martha Graham, who were producing mag-
nificent new works of art well into their nineties. In fact,
scientists have shown that the brain not only does not
lose capacity with age but that in certain ways it ex-
pands. On timed tests done by German researcher Paul
Bates, older subjects were a little slower than younger
ones at such rote tasks as pairing words and places. But
on another task designed to test for wisdom, the people
over sixty scored far higher than any other participants.
Also, neuroscientists Samuel Weiss and Brent Reynolds
at the University of Calgary in Alberta succeeded in stim-
ulating dormant brain cells into renewed activity. Other
studies show that the brain can reactivate itself and that
new synapses, which stimulate electrochemical activity,
are created well past the age of eighty.

Surely, then, a long life is meant to be an active and
worthy one, not merely a marking of time after some
arbitrary benchmark such as mandatory retirement age.
Large corporations may make the mistake of discarding
their wisest and most valuable employees at sixty or
sixty-five, leaving these people with decades to lie fallow,
but you should not make the same mistake. Don't retire
from life just as you reach the peak of your wisdom and
just as you are given the opportunity to pass it on to
your grandchildren. In an interview for the *New York
Times Magazine,* the scientist Lewis Thomas just before
his death said, "The thing we're really good at as a species is usefulness. If we paid more attention to this biological attribute, we'd get a satisfaction that cannot be
obtained from goods or knowledge. If you can contem-
plate the times when you've been useful, even indispen-

sable, to other people, the review of our lives would begin to have effects on the younger generations."

If you've been thinking of spending your retirement years on a beach or a shuffleboard court, please seriously reconsider. Somehow and for some reason, you have received the gift of extra years. The way that you use this gift is critical to the future of humanity. A long life is for learning all that you can and bestowing this knowledge upon the souls of children. As nature extends our family, we need to celebrate the fact that we have an unprecedented plethora of people to help one another and to deal with the myriad problems of this planet. Your family needs you, the world needs you, and you are far too vigorous and valuable to fritter away this precious gift of extra time on earth. The very fact that you don't look or act or feel like the grandparents of even a generation ago does not mean that you are less, but that you are more—in effect, an evolved form of grandparents, primed to do a bigger and more challenging job than any group before you. Glance in the mirror, and you see a person who doesn't "look like a grandparent." But listen to your inner urges, and you will find that your "grandparent hunger," your biological need to be a grandparent and to do the best job possible in that vital role, is as insistent as it has been for all people in all places and all times. So gird yourself for the tasks ahead of you. This is definitely not the moment to climb into an RV and drive away from those who need you.

True, you've been working hard all your lives. You were good kids, devoted parents, dedicated spouses and family people. Yet now, as you become the nation's elders, you are being challenged to be more than any grandparent generation before you. Continue giving—to your children, to your grandchildren, and to society. You have yet another job to do, that of helping your families and society in this constantly evolving world.

To do this job, grandparents must realize that there is no permanent time-out in life. It is a continuum of existence that is always bittersweet, that shifts and changes, that is wonderful at one moment and terrible at another. One thing is sure, it never stays the same. Change is the essence of life, and so is growth. That, in the end, is what this book is about: growth at a new time in life, a time when you may have thought that growth was over.

With time, you and your fellow members of this generation will become less and less bewildered about who you are and what you are about. You will come to grips with your new identity, begin to define and establish your place within the family, and feel more confident about your roles in society. If you become involved in difficult situations, you will be armed with a new sense of importance and a strong identity that will enable you to begin to reknit your family. And perhaps those who have relinquished or lost their grandparenthood will strive to heal their relationships.

Your relationships with your grandchildren and your own children are extremely important, as are all grandparent/parent/grandchild and elder/midlife/child relationships. Your roles as a grandparent are not only dependent on you yourself and the culture in which you live, but are deeply and inexorably rooted in human nature. All of us must fulfill these roles for the benefit of the young. It is easy to lose out on the responsibilities and joys of grandparenthood. Don't let it to happen to you.

Think of your family as a large, complex network of

loving people that is made distinct by the idiosyncrasies of its members and made strong by its diversity. We should not view ourselves merely as a nation of individuals but as a nation of families, and this should be reflected in our attitudes, our cultural trends, our national values, and our laws.

Every psychiatrist and psychotherapist can tell you that happiness is a direct result of positive emotional attachments to others. The grandparent/grandchild relationship is one of the most easily accessible reservoirs of joy. I hope that you will come to see your own relationship with your grandchildren that way. I hope that you see yourself as part of a family that reaches far and wide, and that you will play an important role in piecing together your own family network.

We also need to work together to convince our judicial system that it must move away from its hands-off approach toward family strife to a more aggressive role as a force to initiate the healing of family wounds, and to include in that role the development of systems and institutions that can collaborate with the mental health professions to appropriately serve families.

And one final direct appeal to you, the new breed of grandparents: Find your grandparenthood among all of your diverse identities. Try to give it priority. Reassess your goals, and see if you can make more room for your family in them. Love your family, and help your family. Do the same for your community and society. And rescind what I call the New Social Contract that has caused so many grandparents to drop out of life.

If ever the world needed active and effective grandparents, it's now. As a member of the new generation of grandparents, you should ask the best of yourself. Your grandparent years should not be a period of impaired functioning, whether physical or mental. Take advantage of the new knowledge and wisdom about aging and do everything you can to maintain the vital connection between the elder and younger generations, and to share your wisdom and spiritual knowledge. This achievement will be the reward for your lifetime quest for a state of intellectual, emotional, and spiritual maturity and will assure the continuity of your legacy, thus preventing the disappearance of all you have become in your lifetime. Your evolving life view will grant you an increasingly selfless orientation and a lessening of your investment in earthly things. With this new state comes a burst of self-confidence which frees you to behave in positive and constructive ways, bestowing kindness and concern on your family, and in concert with your cohort, on the world at large. You will find that you are more capable than you had ever imagined of making a significant contribution to humanity. You will also find that whatever the complexities of your life and the life of your family, you can achieve a mutually joyous and loving bond with your children, your children's children, and in all probability your great-grandchildren as well.

And that, after all, is what a long life is for.

Appendix

GRANDPARENT RESOURCES

The following organizations deal with different aspects of grandparenting interests, programs, and activities. They offer advice and guidance. Those with an asterisk (*) offer newsletters. I am familiar with these organizations and the dedicated people who run them. If you are interested in what they do and how they do it, feel free to write to them.

GENERAL ORGANIZATIONS

Creative Grandparenting*
Robert Kasey
609 Blackgates Rd.
Wilmington, DE 19803

This organization sponsors a series of programs and projects aimed at promoting positive grandparenting. A key program uses grandparents as mentors in the community. For a sample copy of the newsletter, write to the above address.

Foundation for Grandparenting*
Arthur Kornhaber, M.D.
Box 326
Cohasset, MA 02025

Established in 1980, this is a nonprofit organization dedicated to promoting the importance of grandparents and grandparenting activities for the betterment of grandchildren, families, and society. The foundation publishes a quarterly newsletter, "Vital Connections," engages in intergenerational research projects in conjunction with the St. Francis Academy, and operates a summer camp for grandparents and grandchildren in the Adirondacks. It was also instrumental in establishing grandparent visitation laws and, in collaboration with Generations United, convened the First National Grandparent Conference in 1992. Another conference is in the planning stages. If you would like more information and a complimentary copy of the newsletter, send a stamped (52¢), legal-sized, self-addressed envelope to the above address.

Grandparent Classes: Becoming a Better Grandparent
and Achieving Grandparent Potential
Shirley and Robert Strom
College of Education
Arizona State University
Tempe, AZ 85287-0611

Grandparents Little Dividends
Young Grandparents Clubs*
Sunie Levin
P.O. Box 1143
Shawnee Mission, KS 66207

Request information on groups in your area, and a sample copy of the newsletter, which is full of tips for good grandparenting.

The Joy of Grandparenting
Clarice A. Orr
7100 Old Post Rd. #20
Lincoln, NE 68506

This organization sponsors a nationwide network of classes in effective grandparenting. Write for information on classes in your area.

National Federation of Grandmothers Clubs of America
203 N. Wabash Ave.
Chicago, IL 60601

This is the oldest existing grandparent organization in the country. It is devoted primarily to charitable and volunteer activities.

Too Faraway Grandparents Newsletter
Mike Moldovan
P.O. Box 71
Del Mar, CA 92014

Moldevan, seventy-two, fills his newsletter with practical tips on how to keep in touch with dispersed grandchildren. He explains, "Stereotypes aside, elders offer the young no-charge affection, understanding, and eventually, when the affection is mutual, role models; youngsters provide the elderly with sincerity, stimulation, and a chunk of their infectious love of life." Send for a sample copy.

INTERGENERATIONAL PROGRAMS

Administration on Aging
Dr. Joyce T. Berry, Commissioner
Room 4760, Cohen Building
330 Independence Ave. SW
Washington, DC 20201

Catholic Services to the Elderly
Sister Francene Merkosky OLVM
7900 NE Second Ave.
Miami, FL 33138

Center for Family Education
Dr. Helene Block
Oakton Community College
7701 N. Lincoln
Skokie, IL 60077

Florida Center for Children and Youth
Jack Levine, Executive Director

Box 6646
Tallahassee, FL 32314

Foster Grandparents
330 Independence Ave. SW
Washington, DC 20201

Gatekeepers to the Future
Marty Knowlton
Fort Cronkhite Building 1055
Sausalito, CA 94965

Generations Together
Dr. Sallie Newman
University Center for Social and Urban Research
600A Thackery Hall
University of Pittsburgh
Pittsburgh, PA 15260

Generations United
Tess Scannell
440 First St. NW #310
Washington, DC 20001

House Select Committee on Aging
715 O'Neill House Office Building
Washington, DC 20515

Menninger Child Care Center
Kathleen Leon, Director
5301 West Seventh
Topeka, KS 66606

A publication entitled "Grandparenting—The Intergenerational Connection" can be obtained upon request. There is a catalog of grandparent/grandchild activities, a section called Grandparenting Curriculum Ideas, and a list of resource materials.

National Council on Aging
Intergenerational Projects
Miriam Charnow, Director

600 Maryland Ave. SW
West Wing 100
Washington, DC 20201

The NCOA sponsors programs matching volunteers fifty-five and over with disabled children twelve and younger.

National Intergenerational Week
Fred Ramstedt
350 Arballo Dr. 10-J
San Francisco, CA 94132

New Age Inc.
Carol H. Tice, Director
1212 Roosevelt
Ann Arbor, MI 48014

Dr. Tice pioneered intergenerational activities in school settings and developed TLC—Teaching/Learning Communities. New Age Inc. is dedicated to intergenerational education, service, and research. The organization provides technical consultation and intergenerational curricula and materials in addition to sponsoring conferences and workshops. Several publications and videotapes are available.

Stagebridge—A Senior Theater Company
Stuart Kandell, Director
2501 Harrison St.
Oakland, CA 94612

St. Francis Academy
Mary Lou Calhoun
509 East Elm Street
Salina, KS 67401

A clinical program which uses grandparents to enhance family well-being and heal problems.

GRANDPARENTS' RIGHTS AND CHILDREN'S
ADVOCACY ORGANIZATIONS

Gramps—Grandparents Rights Advocacy Group
Pat and Jack Slorah
1225 North Florida Ave.
Tarpon Springs, Fl 34689

Grandchildren's Rights to Grandparents
237 S. Catherine
La Grange, IL 60525

Grandparents
Ethel Evans
Box 945
Big Bear Lake, CA 92315

Grandparents Against Immorality and Neglect
Betty Parbs
720 Kingston Place
Shreveport, LA 71108

Grandparents Care
Marty Smith
344 S. Columbine Circle
Englewood, CO 80110

Grandparents'-Children's Rights of Missouri
Ann Conkwright
424 E. Stanford
Springfield, MO 65807

Grandparents'-Grandchildren's Rights
Lee and Lucille Sumpter
5728 Bayonne Ave.
Haslett, MI 48840

Grandparents Inc. of Central New Jersey
Alice Everett-Abner
P.O. Box 244
Piscataway, NJ 08854-0244

Grandparents of Pennsylvania
R.R.1
East Brady, PA 16028

Grandparents Reaching Out
141 Glensummer Rd.
Holbrook, NY 11741

Grandparents Rights Organization
Richard S. Victor
555 S. Woodward Ave. #600
Birmingham, MI 48009

Grandparents United for Children's Rights
Ethel Dunn
137 Larkin St.
Madison, MI 53705

Grandparents Who Care
Doriane Miller, M.D./Sue Tropin, R.N.
P.O. Box 245
San Francisco, CA 94124

Maryland Grandparents for Children's Rights
Linda Kelley, Director
7811 Flint Hill Rd.
Owings, MD 20736

Orphaned Grandparents Association of Edmonton
The Family Centre
9912-106 St., 3rd floor
Edmonton, Alberta, CN T5K 1C5

Scarsdale Family Counseling Center*
Edith Engel, Marjorie Slavin
405 Harwood Building
Scarsdale, NY 10583

Publishes the "Grandparent's Newsletter" for grandparents in divided
families.

Grandparents Raising Grandchildren

The number of state and national support groups for grandparents raising their grandchildren is increasing.

Grandparents As Parents (GAP)
Sylvie de Toledo
Psychiatric Clinic for Youth
2801 Atlantic Ave.
Long Beach, CA 90801

Grandparents Raising Grandchildren
Barbara Kirkland, Chairperson
P.O. Box 104
Colleyville, TX 76034

The National Grandparent Information Center
Social Outreach and Support Center
601 E Street NW
Washington, DC 20049
(202) 434-2296

ROCKING (Raising Our Children's Kids)
Box 96
Niles, MI 49120

School of Public Health
Prof. Meredith Minkler
University of California, Berkeley
Berkeley, CA 94720

Second Time Around Parents
Michele Daly
Family and Community Services of Delaware County
100 W. Front St.
Media, PA 19063

Books

Grandparents-Grandchildren: The Vital Connection, by Arthur Kornhaber, M.D., and Kenneth Woodward (New Brunswick, N.J.: Transaction Press, 1985), 12 Sheldon Road, Cohasset, MA 02025. $18.95.

Grandchildren Visitation Disputes: A Legal Resource Manual ($19.95 + $2.95 postage and handling), ABA Order Fulfillment, 750 Lake Shore Drive, Chicago, IL 60611.

Intergenerational Handbook, published by the Intergenerational Activities Program, Broome County Child Development Council, 29 Fayette St. P.O. Box 880, Binghamton, NY 13902-0880. $22.50.

The Rights of Older Persons: A Basic Guide to the Rights of Older Persons Under Current Law, by Robert H. Brown with legal counsel for the elderly. An American Civil Liberties Union Handbook, published by the Southern Illinois University Press, 1989. $7.95.

Bibliography

Aldrich, Robert A., and Glenn Austin. *Grandparenting for the Nineties.* Escondido, Calif.: Erdmann Publishing, 1991.

Allred, G. B., and J. E. Dobson. "Remotivation Group Interaction: Increasing Children's Contact with the Elderly." *Elementary School Guidance and Counseling* 21 (1987).

Apple, David. "The Social Structure of Grandparenthood." *American Anthropologist* 58 (1956).

Areen, Judith. Statement, Hearing before the Subcommittee on Human Services, Select Committee on Aging. House of Representatives. Washington, D.C., December 16, 1982.

Arria, Amelia M., et al. "The Effects of Alcohol Abuse on the Health of Adolescents." *Alcohol Health and Research World* 15:1 (1991).

Baranowski, Mark M.D. "Grandparent Adolescent Relations: Beyond the Nuclear Family." *Adolescence* 15 (1982).

Bartlett, Cody B. *Staying Fit Past Fifty.* Indianapolis: Masters Press, 1992.

Belin, David W. *Leaving Money Wisely: Creative Estate Planning for Middle- and Upper-Income Americans for the 1990s.* New York: Charles Scribner's Sons, 1990.

Bengston, Vern L. "Diversity and Symbolism in Grandparent Roles." In Vern L. Bengston and Joan F. Robertson, eds., *Grandparenthood.* Beverly Hills, Calif.: Sage Publications, 1985.

———, et al. "Multigeneration Family Concepts and Findings." In Garms-Homolva, et al., eds., *Intergenerational Relationships.* New York: G. J. Hogrefe, 1984.

Berg, Adriane G. *Making Up for Lost Time: How to Reclaim Your Wealthy Future.* New York: William Morrow, 1991.

Blackwelder, D. E., and R. E. Passman. "Grandmother's and Mother's Disciplining in Three-Generational Families." *Journal of Personality and Social Psychology* 50:1 (1986).

Blazer D. "Current Concepts: Depression in the Elderly." *New England Journal of Medicine* 320:3 (1989).

Bowen, Murray. "A Family Concept of Schizophrenia." In D. D. Jackson, ed., *Etiology of Schizophrenia.* New York: Basic Books, 1960.

———. *Family Therapy in Clinical Practice.* New York: Jason Aronson, 1978.

Bower, B. "Marked Questions on Elderly Depression." *Science News* 140:20 (1991).

Boyd-Franklin, Nancy. *Black Families in Therapy: A Multisystems Approach.* New York: Guilford Press, 1989.

Bronfenbrenner, Urie. *The Ecology of Human Development: Experiments by Nature and Design.* Cambridge, Mass.: Harvard University Press, 1981.

———. *Two Worlds of Children.* New York: Russell Sage, 1970.

Brookdale Grandparent Caregiver Information Project. University of California, 1992.

Buchanan, B., and J. Lappin. "Restoring the Soul of the Family." *Family Therapy Networker,* Nov./Dec. 1990.

Bumagin, V., and K. Hirn. "Observations on Changing Relationships for Older Married Women." *American Journal of Psychoanalysis* 42: 2 (1982).

Butler, Robert N., and Myrna I. Lewis. *Aging and Mental Health: Positive Psychological Approaches.* St. Louis: C.V. Mosby Company, 1973.

Caren, L. D. "Effects of Exercise on the Human Immune System." *Bioscience* 41:6 (1991).

Carter, Stephen L. *The Culture of Disbelief: How American Law and Politics Trivialize Religious Devotion.* New York: Basic Books, 1993.

Cerrato, P. L. "Does Diet Affect the Immune System?" *RN* 53:6, (1990).

Chairman Reports, Subcommittee on Human Services. *Grandparents: New Roles and Responsibilities,* Comm. Pub. No. 102–876. *Grandparents Rights: A Resource Manual,* Comm. Pub. No. 102–898.

Cherlin, Andrew, and Frank F. Furstenberg, Jr. "Grandparents and Family Crisis." *Generations* 10:4 (1986).

————. *The New American Grandparent: A Place in the Family, a Life Apart.* New York: Basic Books, 1986.

Chopra, Deepak. *Ageless Body, Timeless Mind: The Quantum Alternative to Growing Old.* New York: Harmony Books, 1993.

Cohler, Bertram J. *Mothers, Grandmothers, and Daughters.* New York: John Wiley & Sons, 1981.

Coles, Robert. The Old Ones of New Mexico. Albuquerque: University of New Mexico Press, 1973.

Consumer's Guide. Vitamins for a Healthy Life. Skokie, Ill., 1987.

Costanzo, Christie, with Leo Costanzo. *Mommy and Me Exercises: The Kidnastics Program.* Sacramento: Cougar Books, 1983.

Department of Health and Environment, State of Kansas. Department of Health and Human Services, Administration for Children and Families, July 1992.

"Does Exercise Boost Immunity?" University of California, Berkeley Wellness Letter 8:6.

Erikson, Erik H. *Childhood and Society*. New York: W.W. Norton, 1963.

——. *The Life Cycle Completed: A Review*. New York: W.W. Norton, 1982.

——, et al. *Vital Involvement in Old Age: The Experience of Old Age in Our Time*. New York: W.W. Norton, 1986.

Etzioni, Amitai. *The Spirit of Community: Rights, Responsibilities and the Communitarian Agenda*. New York: Crown Publishers, 1993.

Foster, Robert, and Doris Freed. "Grandparent Visitation: Vagaries and Vicissitudes." *Journal of Divorce* 70:1/2 (fall/winter 1979).

Fox, Arnold, M.D., and Barry Fox. *Immune for Life: Live Longer and Better by Strengthening Your Doctor Within*. Rocklin, Calif.: Prima Publishing, 1989.

Freedman, Michael. "Fostering Intergenerational Relationships for At-Risk Youths." *Children Today* 18:2 (1989).

Friedan, Betty. *The Fountain of Age*. New York: Simon & Schuster, 1993.

Furstenberg, Frank F., Jr., and Andrew J. Cherlin. *Divided Families: What Happens to Children When Parents Part*. Cambridge, Mass.: Harvard University Press, 1991.

Furstenberg, Frank F., Jr., and Graham B. Spanier. *Recycling the American Family After Divorce*. Beverly Hills, Calif: Sage Publications, 1984.

Germani, C. "Caring for 'Orphans of the Living.' *Christian Science Monitor*, August 13, 1990.

Gilligan, Carol. *In a Different Voice: Psychological Theory and Women's Development*. Cambridge, Mass.: Harvard University Press, 1982.

Glover, Rob, and Jack Shepherd. *The Family Fitness Handbook*. New York: Penguin Books, 1989.

Gluckin, Doreen, M.D. *The Body at Thirty*. New York: M. Evans and Company, 1982.

Golden R. N., et al. "Circulating Natural Killer Phenotypes in Men and

Women with Major Depression: Relation to Cytotoxic Activity and Severity of Depression." *Archives of General Psychiatry* 49 (1992).

Greenburg, J. S., and M. Becker. "Aging Parents as Family Resources." *The Gerontologist* 28:6 (1988).

Guerin, Philip, and K. B. Guerin. "Theoretical Aspects and Clinical Relevance of the Multigenerational Model of Family Therapy." In Guerin, et al., *Family Therapy Theory and Practice.* New York: Gardner Press, 1976.

Gutmann, David. "Personhood and the Life Course." In Vern L. Bengston and Joan F. Robertson, eds., *Grandparenthood.* Beverly Hills, Calif.: Sage Publications, 1985.

———. *Reclaimed Powers: Toward a New Psychology of Men and Women in Later Life.* New York: Basic Books, 1987.

Hagestad, Gunhild O. "Continuity and Connectedness." In Vern L. Bengston and Joan F. Robertson, eds., *Grandparenthood.* Beverly Hills, Calif.: Sage Publications, 1985.

———. "Demographic Change and the Life Course: Some Emerging Trends in the Family Realm." *Family Relations* 37 (1988).

Higgans, P. S., and R. Faunce. *Attitudes of Minneapolis Elementary Schools and Senior Citizens Toward Each Other.* Minneapolis: Minneapolis Public Schools, Department of Research and Evaluation, C-76-34. (March 1977).

Hines, P. "The Family Life Cycle of Poor Black Families." In B. Caret and M. McGoldrick, eds., *The Changing Family Life Cycle: A Framework for Family Therapy.* 2nd ed. Boston: Allyn and Bacon, 1989.

Jendrek, Margaret P. *Grandparents Who Parent Their Grandchildren.* AARP, Andrus Foundation, 1993.

Johnson, C. "A Cultural Analysis of the Grandmother." *Research in Aging* 5:4 (1983).

Jones, Ernest. *The Life and Work of Sigmund Freud.* New York: Basic Books, 1957.

Josephy, Alvin M., Jr. *The Indian Heritage of America.* New York: Bantam Books, 1968.

Kahana, B., and E. Kahana "Grandparenthood from the Perspective of the Developing Grandchild." *Developmental Psychology* 3 (1972).

Kahana, E., and B. Kahana. "Theoretical and Reseach Perspectives on Grandparenthood." *Aging and Human Development* 2 (1971).

Kaufman, Nona, Naomi Lederach, and Beth Lederach. *Exercise as You Grow Older*. Intercourse, Pa.: Good Books, 1986.

Kellam, S. G., et al. "Family Structure and the Neonatal Health of Children." *Archives of General Psychiatry* 34 (1977).

Kennedy, J. F., and V. T. Keeny. "The Extended Family Revisited: Grandparents Rearing Grandchildren." *Child Psychiatry and Human Development* 19 (1988).

———. "Group Psychotherapy with Grandparents Rearing Their Emotionally Disturbed Grandchildren." *Group* 11:1 (1987).

Kidder, Tracy. *Old Friends*. New York: Houghton Mifflin, 1993.

Kivnick, Helen Q. "Grandparenthood: An Overview of Meaning and Mental Health." *Gerontologist* 22 (1982).

———. "Grandparenthood: Life Review and Psychosocial Development." *Journal of Gerontological Social Work* 12:3/4 (1988).

———. *The Meaning of Grandparenthood*. Ann Arbor, Mich.: UMI Press, 1980.

Kornhaber, Arthur, M.D. "America's Forgotten Resource: Grandparents." *U.S. News & World Report*, June 1984.

———. "Are Your Children Problem Parents?" *Grandparents* 2 (fall 1987).

———. *Between Parents & Grandparents*. New York: St. Martin's Press, 1986.

———. "Bringing Young and Old Together: Intergenerational Programs." *Natural Health*, May 1993.

———. "Grandparenting, Normal and Pathological." *American Journal of Geriatric Psychiatry*, 1986.

———. "Grandparents and Infants." *French Journal of Child Psychiatry*, June 1989.

———. "Grandparents Are Coming of Age in America." *Children Today*, July 1983.

———. "Les Grands-parents: Le Monde du bébé." In Serge Lebovici and Paul Weil-Halpern. Paris: Presse Medicale, 1990.

――――. "Grandparents: The Other Victims of Divorce." *Reader's Digest*, February 1983.

――――. "Infants and Grandparents." In Evelyn Rexford, et al., *Infant Psychiatry*. New Haven: Yale University Press, 1989.

――――. "The New Social Contract: Grandparenthood." In Vern L. Bengston et al., Beverly Hills, Calif.: Sage Publications, 1988.

――――. *Proceedings of the World Congress of Child Psychiatry*. Paris, 1986.

――――. "Raising Grandchildren." *Vital Connections* 14 (spring 1993).

――――. The Vital Connection Between the Old and the Young. The Birth of the Intergenerational Movement in America. Address. Administration On Aging National Meeting. 1982.

――――, et al. *Spirit: Mind, Body and the Will to Existence*. New York: St. Martin's Press, 1989.

――――. "Talking to God." *Newsweek*, January 1992.

――――. "What It Really Means to Grandparent." *Grandparents*, summer 1988.

――――, and H. Benson. "Reductions in Negative Psychological Characteristics with a New Relaxation Response Health Curriculum In High School Students." *Behavioral Medicine*, 1993.

Kornhaber, Arthur, M.D., and Kenneth L. Woodward. "Bringing Back Grandma." *Newsweek*, May 1981.

――――. *Grandparents-Grandchildren: The Vital Connection*. New York: Doubleday, 1981.

――――. *Grand-Parents, Petits-Enfants: Le Lien Vital*. Paris: Robert Laffont, 1985.

Krause, Corinne. *Grandmothers, Mothers and Daughters: Oral Histories of Three Generations of Ethnic American Women*. New York: Macmillan, 1991.

Kunstler, James. *The Geography of Nowhere: The Rise and Decline of America's Man-Made Landscape*. New York: Simon & Schuster, 1993.

Lambert, D. J., et al. "Planning for Contact Between the Generations: An Effective Approach." *The Gerontologist* 30:4 (1990).

Lynch, James J. *The Broken Heart: Medical Consequences of Loneliness.* New York: Basic Books, 1976.

———. *The Language of the Heart: The Human Body in Dialogue.* New York: Basic Books, 1985.

Maslow, Abraham. *Toward a Psychology of Being.* New York: Van Nostrand Reinhold, 1968.

Matthews, Sara H., and Jetse Sprey. "The Impact of Divorce on Grandparenthood: An Exploratory Study." *The Gerontologist* 24 (February 1984).

McCready, William C. "The Persistence of Ethnic Variation in American Families." In A. W. Greeley and W. C. McCready, eds., *Ethnicity in the United States.* New York: Wiley-Interscience, 1974.

———. "Styles of Grandparenting Among White Ethnics." In Vern L. Bengston and Joan F. Robertson, eds., *Grandparenthood.* Beverly Hills, Calif.: Sage Publications, 1985.

McGoldrick, Monica, et al., *Ethnicity and Family Therapy.* New York: Guilford Press, 1982.

Mead, Margaret. *Blackberry Winter: My Earlier Years.* New York: William Morrow, 1972.

Minckler, Meredith, and Kathleen M. Roe. *Grandmothers as Caregivers.* Newbury Park, Calif.: Sage Press, 1993.

Montemayor, R., and G. K. Leigh. "Parent-Absent Children: A Demographic Analysis of Children and Adolescents Living Apart from Their Parents." *Family Relations* 31 (1982).

Moody, H. R., and R. Disch. "Intergenerational Programming in Public Policy." *Journal of Children in Contemporary Society.* 20:3/4 (1989).

Mugerauer, Robert. "Professors as Grandparents." *Grand Valley College Review,* spring 1974.

Nahenow, N. "The Changing Nature of Grandparenthood." *Medical Aspects of Human Sexuality* 19:4 (1985).

National Association Perinatal Addiction Resource, 1990.

Neugarten, Bernice L., and Carol K. Weinstein. "The Changing American Grandparent." *Journal of Marriage and the Family* 26 (1964).

Newman, S., and S. W. Brummel. *Intergenerational Programs*. New York: Haworth Press, 1989.

Newman, Sally. "A History of Intergenerational Programs." *Journal of Children in Contemporary Society*. 20:3/4 (1989).

Oliver, J. E. "Intergenerational Transmission of Child Abuse: Rates, Research and Clinical Implications." *American Journal of Psychiatry* 150 (1993).

Ostroff, J. "Intergenerational Marketing." *Marketing Communications* 14:5 (1989).

Paulme, Denise. *Women of Tropical Africa*. Los Angeles: Mouton & Co., University of California Press, 1960.

Peterson, Christopher. *Health and Optimism*. New York: Free Press, 1991.

Poe, Lenora M. "Black Grandparents As Parents: Preventing Elderly Suicide." *The Futurist* 25:5 (1991).

Rakoff, V. M., and Lefebvre, A. "Conjoint Family Therapy." In R. G. Hirschowitz and B. Levy, eds., *The Changing Mental Health Scene*. New York: Spectrum, 1976.

Rappaport, E. A. "The Grandparent Syndrome." *Psychoanalytic Quarterly* 27 (1958).

Rathbone-McCuan, E., and R. Pierce. "Intergenerational Treatment Approach: An Alternative Model of Working with Abusive/Neglectful and Delinquent Prone Families." *Family Therapy* 5:2 (1978).

Robertson, Joan F. "Grandmotherhood: A Study of Role Conception." *Journal of Marriage and the Family* 39 (1977).

———. "Significance of Grandparents: Perceptions of Young Adult Grandchildren." *Gerontologist* 16:2 (1976).

Rosenthal, C. Julian, and V. W. Marshall. "The Head of the Family: Authority and Responsibility in the Lineage." Paper presented at the annual meeting of the Gerontological Society of America, 1983.

Rothenbuhler, E. W. "The Process of Community Involvement." *Communication Monographs* 58:1 (1991).

Ryan, V. C., and M. E. Bower. "Relationship of Socioeconomic Status and Living Arrangements to Nutritional Intake of the Older Person." *Journal of the American Dietetic Association* 89:12 (1989).

Sartre, Jean-Paul. *The Words,* trans. Bernard Frechtman. New York: Faucett World Library, 1977.

Saltzman, G. A. "Grandparents Raising Grandchildren." *Creative Grandparenting,* 2:4 (1992).

Schultz, A. *The Phenomenology of the Social World.* Chicago: Northwestern University Press, 1967.

Shanas, E. "Older People and Their Families: The New Pioneers." *Journal of Marriage and the Family* 42 (1980).

Singer, Dr. Jerome L. *The House of Make-Believe.* Cambridge, Mass.: Harvard University Press, 1991.

Sprey, Jetse, and Sara H. Matthews. "Contemporary Grandparenthood: A Systematic Transition." *Annals of the American Academy of Political Science* 464 (1982).

Stamm, K. R., and L. Fortini-Campbell. "The Relationship of Community." *Journalism Monographs* 84 (1983).

Stokes, J., and J. Greenstone. "Helping Black Grandparents and Older Parents Cope with Child Rearing: A Group Method." *Child Welfare* 60 (1981).

Stone, E. "Mothers and Daughters." *Parents Magazine* 66:5 (1991).

Strom, Robert D., and Shirley K. Strom. *Achieving Grandparent Potential.* Newbury Park, Calif.: Sage Publications, 1991.

———. *Becoming a Better Grandparent.* Newbury Park, Calif.: Sage Publications, 1991.

Strom, Robert, et al. "Strengths and Needs of Black Grandparents." *International Journal of Aging and Human Development* 36:4 (1992/93).

Timberlake, E. M., and S. Chipunga. "Grandmotherhood: Contemporary Meaning Among African-American Middle-Class Grandmothers." *Social Work* 37:3 (1992).

Strauss, C. A. "Grandma Made Johnny Delinquent." *American Journal of Orthopsychiatry* 13 (1943).

Thomas, Alexander, et al. *Temperament and Behavior Disorders in Children.* New York: New York University Press, 1968.

Troll, Lillian E. "Grandparents: The Family Watchdogs." In T. Brubaker, ed., *Family Relationships in Later Life.* Beverly Hills, Calif.: Sage Publications, 1983.

United States Department of Commerce, Bureau of the Census. *Statistical Abstract of the United States.* Washington, D.C: U.S. Government Printing Office, 1990.

Van Hentig, Hans. "The Social Function of the Grandmother." *Social Forces* 24 (1946).

Victor, Richard S. Statement at Hearing before the Subcommittee on Human Services, Select Committee on Aging, U.S. House of Representatives, Washington, D.C., December 16, 1982.

Vollmer, H. "The Grandmother: A Problem in Child Rearing." *American Journal of Orthopsychiatry* 7 (1973).

Wechsler, Harlan J. "Judaic Perspectives on Grandparenthood." In Vern L. Bengston and Joan F. Robertson, eds., *Grandparenthood.* Beverly Hills: Sage Publications, 1985.

Whitaker, Carl A. *A Family Is a Four-Dimensional Relationship: Family Therapy Theory and Practice.* New York: Gardner Press, 1976.

White, Linda B. *The Grandparent Book: Thoroughly Modern Grandparenting.* San Francisco: Gateway Books, 1990.

Wilson, K. B., and M. R. DeShare. "The Legal Right of Grandparents: A Preliminary Discussion." *Gerontologist* 22 (1982).

Winslow, R. "Questionnaire Probes Patients' Quality of Life." *Wall Street Journal,* July 7, 1992.

Wood, V., and Joan F. Robertson. "The Significance of Grandparenthood." In Jaber F. Gubrium, ed., *Time, Roles and Self in Old Age.* New York: Human Sciences Press, 1976.

Wilcoxon, A. "Grandparents and Grandchildren: An Often Neglected Relationship Between Significant Others." *Journal of Counseling and Development* 65 (1987).

Acknowledgments

This book is the result of the vision and work of a host of people whom I would like to thank for their efforts and their friendship.

First and foremost, I would like to thank all of the people who have taken part in the Grandparent Study, now well into its third decade. It is a privilege to know such wonderful people. Their stories fill these pages. Of course, names and places have been changed to ensure confidentiality.

I want to thank members of my family who are my partners in the everyday reality of family life that I study and write about. My love and thanks to my wife, Carol Kornhaber, executive director of the Foundation for Grandparenting, who has co-directed the Grandparent Study with me and contributed greatly to this work. I also want to express my love and thanks to my grandsons, Justin and Tyler, and their parents, Sabra and Jay Goodman, for teaching me how to be a mature father and neophyte grandfather in the real world.

I would also like to express my love and thanks to my son, David Kornhaber, who collaborated with me in a different version of this work. In addition to his considerable conceptual and literary talents, David brought the important perspective of the under-thirty generation to the work. My love and thanks to my daughters, Chantal and Mila, who weren't directly involved in the project but offered helpful advice and perspective.

I want to thank members of my "professional" family, which created this work. My thanks and affection to my literary agent, Loretta Barrett, for her belief in this work and her creative efforts as a "producer" to make it happen. Most of all, I want to thank Loretta for being a caring, kind, and spirited friend ever since we did our first book together. Thanks also to my gifted editor at Crown, Betty Prashker, who, with professional vision and as a grandmother personally familiar with the topic, brings this book into the world.

The highlight of working on this book was collaborating with Sondra Forsyth, a woman brilliant in mind and spirit. Sondra has become a valued friend. My thanks and affection to Sondra's daughter, Stacey, too. Stacey had plenty of ideas and stories to offer while her mother and I worked on the manuscript. Sondra's views and spirit live in these pages.

Index